Edexcel A2 Music Technology Revision Guide

David Ventura

D0177198

R· RHINEGOLD
EDUCATION

www.rhinegoldeducation.co.uk

Music Study Guides

GCSE, AS and A2 Music Study Guides (AQA, Edexcel and OCR)

GCSE, AS and A2 Music Listening Tests (AQA, Edexcel and OCR)

GCSE, AS and A2 Music Revision Guides (AQA, Edexcel and OCR)

AS/A2 Music Technology Study Guide, Listening Tests and Revision Guides (Edexcel)

Also available from Rhinegold Education

Music Technology from Scratch

Understanding Popular Music

Musicals in Focus, Baroque Music in Focus, Film Music in Focus

Dictionary of Music in Sound

First published 2013 in Great Britain by

Rhinegold Education

14-15 Berners Street

London W1T 3LJ

www.rhinegoldeducation.co.uk

You should always check the current requirements of the examination, since these may change. Copies of the Edexcel specification can be downloaded from the Edexcel website at www.edexcel.com. Edexcel Publications email: publication.orders@edexcel.com, telephone: 01623 467467, fax: 01623 450481

Edexcel A2 Music Technology Revision Guide

Order No. RHG330

ISBN: 978-1-78038-069-8

Exclusive Distributors:

Music Sales Ltd

Distribution Centre, Newmarket Road

Bury St Edmunds, Suffolk IP33 3YB, UK

Printed in the EU

Contents

The author

David Ventura read music at Edinburgh University, has taught music in Scotland, Lancashire, Liverpool and Isle of Wight, and was the director of music at Hereford Sixth Form College for fifteen years up until 2009. He has lectured nationwide on music technology and has advised the UK Government on assessment in the National Curriculum for music at all key stages. He has acted as a consultant for the Qualifications and Curriculum Authority, was chair of the Southern Examining Group's GCSE panel, has examined for a number of boards, and has also run many teacher-training courses for Keynote Education. David has written a number of publications, including Rhinegold's *Film Music in Focus*, co-authoring the Rhinegold KS3 Elements series, and numerous articles for *Classroom Music* magazine. He is a prolific composer and enjoys playing jazz piano.

Acknowledgements

Joseph Skinner, for a young person's perspective.
Elisabeth Boulton and Ben Smith, for their editorial and design expertise.
All the staff at Rhinegold Education, particularly Katharine Allenby for her patient encouragement.

The author and publisher are grateful to the following for permission to use their images
Page 16: Korg.
Page 28 (left): Coleman Audio.
Page 68: the Moog Modular Synthesiser belongs to Mark Rubel at Pogo Studio, Champaign, IL, and was photographed by Mark Smart.

Introduction

This book is designed to serve as revision material for the Edexcel A2 Music Technology examination: unit 4 (6MT04). The exam combines written responses and practical tasks that will test your understanding of the equipment you have used in the preparation of your coursework, both at AS and A2 levels.

> This revision guide can be used as a reference throughout the year. It forms an ideal companion to the *Edexcel AS/A2 Music Technology Study Guide, second edition* by Jonny Martin (Rhinegold Education, 2009) which explains in detail what you need to do during the two-year course.

With the aid of diagrams and annotations, the first section of this revision guide covers the theory and technical language behind music technology. It examines both the usage of modern equipment in an up-to-date studio and the way techniques and hardware and software developed in the past, in order to form a historical perspective for your learning. These two complementary aspects of the subject are clearly reflected in the structure of the exam itself: questions 1–3 and 5 concentrate on the theoretical and practical aspects; question 4 is based around the development of music technology over the years.

Sections 2 and 3 provide advice on how to approach the questions in the exam itself and how to achieve high marks with your answers. It is very easy to miss out on marks under examination pressure through a lack of focus on the question, or conversely over-concentrating on one particular question and running out of time. There are a number of strategies suggested in this revision guide that may help to alleviate these problems.

In general, there are only a few weeks between the coursework deadline dates and the exam. As well as revision, this is the best time to practise examination technique with past papers. Using the revision guide at this time is also useful reference when looking at the mark schemes for these tests.

> **Extra resource**
> *Edexcel AS/A2 Music Technology Listening Tests, second edition* by Alan Charlton and Alec Boulton (Rhinegold Education, 2010).

Section 1: equipment in context

The nature of audio

When an object vibrates in a medium – in air, for example – it causes the molecules to squash together one moment and space out the next. This is called compression and rarefaction.

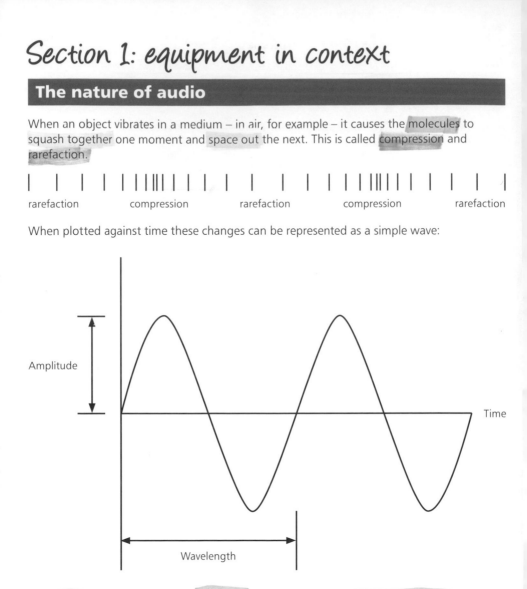

rarefaction   compression   rarefaction   compression   rarefaction

When plotted against time these changes can be represented as a simple wave:

Amplitude

Time

Wavelength

The height of the wave is called amplitude, and the number of peaks and troughs per second is known as frequency, i.e. how frequently the waveform repeats.

In the real world, objects vibrate to produce sound in a more complex way. Pythagoras, a Greek philosopher and mathematician, discovered that strings vibrate in mathematically even sections. Along with the main length (called the fundamental and the perceived pitch), strings also vibrate in two halves, three thirds, four quarters and so on, which became known as harmonics. When the waveforms are added together, a more complex wave is created, which is perceived by the human ear as a new timbre.

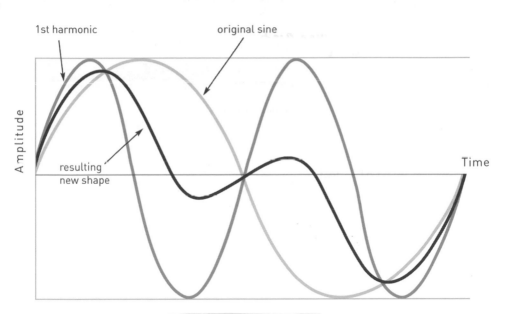

All sound can be regarded as variations in sound pressure. It is simple to think of electronically-produced sound as an analogue copy, where the waveforms are represented by variations in electrical current. The process is a straightforward line when using a microphone to capture the sound:

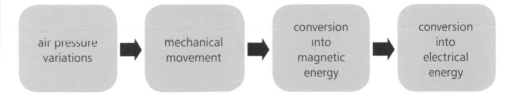

The waveform is then manipulated by the equipment and the reverse line makes it audible:

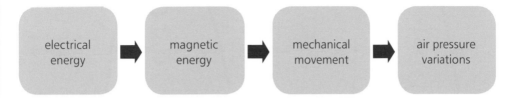

The changes in pressure can be picked up by sensors such as the human eardrum or the diaphragm on a microphone; both of these sensors are flexible enough to move along with the change in pressure.

The engineer in the studio has a number of tools that can be used to manipulate waveforms. For example: filters can remove parts of a waveform; amplifiers can boost a wave's amplitude; low frequency oscillators can apply modulation.

In the digital age, sound is represented by a series of voltages – ons and offs – a system known as binary. This is a language code that computers can work with, which means that the level of control available to engineers to manipulate sound is much higher than before computers became part of the production process. Previously, waveforms were represented physically by patterns engraved on shellac or vinyl material (78 or LP records), or in magnetic imprints on ferric oxide dust stuck to plastic tape (reel-to-reel and cassette tape). With digital music, sound is thousands of on and off messages, controlled by an electronic device.

The process of creating digital music involves taking large numbers of points on the analogue waveform (samples) and encoding this information into binary language. The distance between one sampling point and another is called the sample period. A sample rate of 48kHz corresponds to a time of 48,000 samples every second. To acquire information regarding volume levels or amplitude, the waveform has to be divided into steps (as shown in the diagram diagram below). By increasing the sampling bit depth, quantisation noise is reduced so that the signal-to-noise ratio is improved. In the case of music CDs the number of samples is standardised at 44,100 samples per second with a 16-bit resolution.

In order for us to hear the results, the digital information has to be decoded back into an analogue signal using a digital-to-analogue converter (DAC).

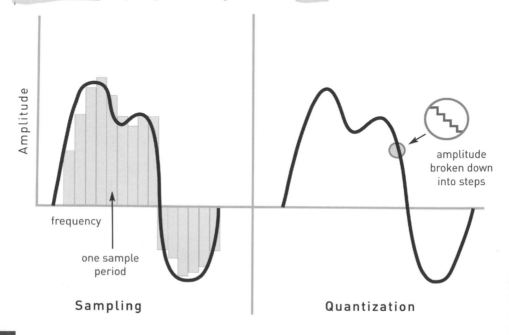

Amplitude

frequency

one sample
period

Sampling

amplitude
broken down
into steps

Quantization

SECTION 1: EQUIPMENT IN CONTEXT

The final processed sound must be raised to a level of audibility, amplified, and sent to a pair of speakers (essentially, like a microphone in reverse). Electrical signals transform through an electromagnet back into mechanical movement – in this case the speaker cone.

The development of audio recording technology

1877	Thomas Edison invented the first machine that could record sound using paraffin-coated paper
1886	Alexander Graham Bell et al invented the graphophone, which uses wax cylinders to record on
1888	Edison invented the phonograph, which made use of an electric motor
1889	Berliner and Suess invented the gramophone, which used a large horn for amplification and flat discs for recording
1898	Valdemar Poulsen patented the first magnetic recording system – a forerunner of tape recording
1901	Mass production of records now possible
1904	Production of Shellac discs in Europe
1927	First 12-inch 40-minute long-playing record available The famous Al Jolson film *The Jazz Singer* was released, with its synchronised sound-to-picture
1931–45	Stereo discs were invented with a different channel of sound inscribed on either side of the V-shaped cut
1936	Jukeboxes were widespread in cafés and bars across the southern United States
1941	Large 16-inch records called V-discs were sent to the troops in World War II, containing a mixture of music
1948	Professional tape recorder manufactured by Ampex Vinyl 33$\frac{1}{3}$ LPs introduced by Columbia Bell labs invented the transistor, enabling much smaller portable systems to be made
1953	Pre-recorded stereo tapes available for use in the home
1957	First stereo discs released
1960	Four-track tape cartridge (two separate stereo tracks) available for cars, featuring a continuous looping system
1963	First compact cassettes available, although these did not become popular for another five years
1966	Eight-track tape systems became a standard option in luxury cars One-inch eight-track recorder introduced by 3M
1966–67	George Martin produced The Beatles' *Sergeant Pepper's Lonely Hearts Club Band*: a landmark in the use of multitrack recording, which combines two four-track tape recorders so that tracks could be bounced down and overdubbed

1968	Ampex introduced 16-track recording
1971	Dolby noise reduction invented, to create reduction in tape hiss
1979	Sony Walkman produced: a portable personalised music-cassette player with headphones
1979	Tascam produced their multitrack cassette 'portastudio' recorder. The cassette was recorded in only one direction so that the normal reverse side could be used for more tracks. To increase the quality of sound, the tape running speed was increased from $1\frac{7}{8}$ inches per second to $3\frac{3}{4}$ inches
1982	CDs produced commercially
1983	Public Image Ltd release *Live in Tokyo*, credited as being the first live album recorded digitally Studios through the 1980s move to digital recording methods
1986	Steinberg releases MIDI recording software 'pro-24' for the Atari – this was to lead to Cubase software and eventually to audio recording on computers **Steinberg Pro-24, the predecessor of Cubase, running on an Atari computer**
1987	DAT (digital audio tape) available – used widely for mastering
1991	Cubase Audio for Mac released
1992	Digital minidisc recording introduced by Sony Soundblaster 16 Pro soundcard enables 16-bit CD quality recording on home computers
1992	ADAT eight-track recording introduced Digital signals were recorded onto highly available VHS (video) tapes
1995	Relatively cheap digital multitrack recorders (standalone and independent of computers with built-in hard drives) became widely available

1997	Virtual studio technology (VST) introduced plug-in effects for processing sound recordings
1997	ATR-1 rack-mounted hardware auto-tune processor released
2001	Apple released the iPod
2003	Legal digital music downloads available through the iTunes store

Recording media

VINYL DISCS

- This format is still in demand today, being noted for its warm sound
- Many dance producers use original vinyl records as their preferred source for sampling
- Vinyl records are collectable items
- Most major record companies have ceased to produce vinyl as it is not as durable or easily editable when compared to digital media; overall it is a more expensive product
- The system works by engraving a copy of an acoustic waveform into a hard but pliable medium such as vinyl. A needle, or stylus, then moves laterally in the groove as the disc is rotated. This mechanical movement can be converted via electromagnetism into sound, aiming to be as close to the original as possible.

ADVANTAGES

- Warm sound
- Easy to locate music (possible to jump sections, unlike having to use fastforward/ rewind on a cassette tape)
- LP cover artwork much admired
- Dance music DJs able to directly manipulate the sound by techniques such as scratching, beatmatching, slip-cuing and controlling the speed of the turntable.

DISADVANTAGES

- Easily damaged through scratching, dirt on the surface or warping
- Repeated playings lead to product wearing out and decrease in clarity
- LPs are bulky and not very portable
- Not fully discrete channel separation
- Pitch variations possible depending on quality of motor for turntable
- Outside electrical interference could be amplified by the magnetic cartridge.

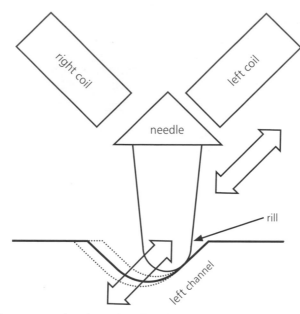

A diagram showing the movement of a stylus on the surface of a record

ANALOGUE TAPE RECORDING

- Particles of ferric oxide (later chromium oxide) coated on polyester strips are arranged in a random pattern until they receive a magnetic signal from the recording head of a tape recorder
- If the signal is musical, the particles become organised into more regular patterns that can be read and played back as an analogue (copy) of the original sound
- An erase head is situated ahead of the record/playback head to facilitate further recording efforts if required, or simply to remove unwanted magnetic signals before recording takes place
- Earlier in the history of tape recording, the record and playback heads were separate, which created a slight delay. Once they became united the possibility of monitoring the original take and recording a new one in time on another parallel track led to multitrack recording. New exciting textures could be produced
- The wider the tape, and the faster it ran, the higher the quality of the reproduction, which offered less background hiss, a better high frequency response and fewer dropouts (audible glitches created by flaws in the magnetic tape). Commercially, two-inch tape was the widest available format.

ADVANTAGES

- The tape medium was relatively cheap (however, because it is no longer mainstream, tape is now very expensive when compared to hard disc recording) Scratches and surface noise were not a problem compared with vinyl records

- Longer recording times than vinyl LPs
- Overdubbing was possible, by recording in new material over a previously recorded track
- Editing was possible by cutting and splicing tape (vinyl does not offer this facility). Beyond correcting errors, cutting and splicing was favoured by creative artists for producing complex collages of sound
- High quality tape could be re-used
- Some elements of distortion could lead to the bass thickening up. Combining such distortion with an in-built high-frequency compression created a natural and warmer sound.

DISADVANTAGES

- The tape had to be wound to the point where the required music could be found. Synchronisation systems helped with this issue in the professional studio: MTC and SMPTE are time codes that are recorded onto a spare track, usually at the edge of the tape, to lock the timing of the tape to other devices)
- There was a hiss produced from the tape, which was removed by various noise reduction technologies such as Dolby B and DBX
- Small pitch variations (known as wow and flutter) can occur depending on the stability of the tape machine's motor
- The tape had to be stored tail out (i.e. wound so that the ending is first) to avoid a magnetic print-through of the encoded signal, which would result in ghostly sounds before the playback began
- Editing was difficult as it required cutting and splicing with razor blades, and was almost impossible with multitracked music.

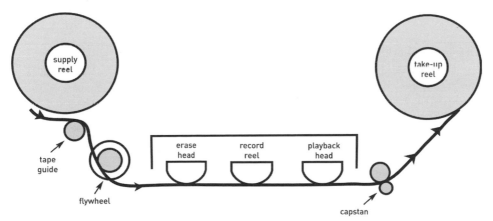

THE COMPACT CASSETTE

Also known as cassette tape, this comprised a length of magnetic tape wound around two miniature reels to transport the tape, all encased in a small plastic box. As only $\frac{1}{8}$ inch wide, the tape could be reversed so each stereo track used only $\frac{1}{16}$ inch of tape, moving at a standard $1\frac{7}{8}$ inches per second. The highest qualities of recording were therefore not available in this medium. However, as the technology improved the compact cassette moved from just office dictation to stereo music and multitracking – although multitracking ran faster and in only one direction to maximise tape area. Cassette tapes were easy to use; in the domestic market they were employed worldwide for making recordings of radio programmes and vinyl records, as well as being sold in their pre-recorded form.

ADVANTAGES

- Highly portable
- Mass-produced and widely available at the time
- Reasonably long record times: the standard C90 tape allowed for 90 minutes, or 45 minutes each side in stereo. Longer times were available but the tape began to be a little thin
- Breaking tabs on the side of the case could protect a recording from erasure, by not allowing the record head to be engaged.

DISADVANTAGES

- Not the highest recording quality because of the narrow width of the tape and the modest speeds of the tape transport. Some manufacturers made equipment with faster speeds for multitrack work, but for compatibility the master tapes would have to be mixed down to standard speeds
- Long length tapes liable to snap
- Recording heads and other areas of the playing equipment needed frequent cleaning because of ferric oxide deposits from the tape.

DIGITAL RECORDING

RAM stands for random access memory as opposed to ROM or read only memory. This is an area in a computer's circuits where information is held only temporarily. It has the advantage that data can be accessed in any order, but the disadvantage that the data is lost when systems are powered down.

- Hard disc recording has gradually replaced tape, and RAM systems replaced hardware multitrack recorders. The ability to quickly access any point in the audio and edit it non-destructively proved a huge advance
- Recordable CDs, useable at home, are now widely available and are able to record audio at higher speeds than real-time
- Digital audio tape (DAT) was favoured in studios, particularly for final mixes in the 1980s and 90s, although nowadays it has been superseded by hard disc recording
- Portable digital recorders were ideal for location recording of concerts, but now are gradually being superseded by laptop computers

- The encoding of analogue signals into binary language, which computers and other chip-based technology can understand, has revolutionised the industry
- Computing capability and memory has become increasingly powerful over the last few decades, with silicon chips that contained hundreds (1960s), millions (1980s) and then billions of transistors
- Software development has taken place alongside new hardware; digital audio recording has moved from specialised equipment to easily installed software packages
- Windows and Mac computers are now the market leaders. Music software is divided into scoring packages such as Sibelius and Finale to complete virtual studios such as Cubase, Logic, Sonar and Reason
- Equipment for capturing audio, taking a microphone or line signal and converting it into digital form has become cheaper and more capable (see page 40 and following for I/O information)
- With the increased computing power of faster processors and larger RAM, it has been possible to produce recordings of CD quality and above, so much so that activities only possible in professional studios in the 70s and 80s can now be carried out on laptops
- Parallel to these developments, portable hard disc recorders emerged
- Through audio compression techniques, digital music transfers over the internet are now the norm; iPods and mobile phones can reproduce music of a very acceptable quality.

OTHER DIGITAL FORMATS

Some digital formats have gone by the wayside. Minidisc, tape ADAT and DAT (digital audio tape) are now used infrequently. DAT was very common as a studio mastering medium and ADAT, because it utilised highly available VHS tapes, was a cost effective multitrack solution.

Minidisc was a highly portable system invented by the Sony Corporation. The discs were only 64mm across and used a rewritable magneto-optical material. During recording a laser beam was used to heat magnetic material, which changed its characteristics. An electromagnet could then read these changes. A minidisc could record up to 74 minutes of audio but had to use Sony's audio compression format (ATRAC), so like MP3 some of the sound was lost.

DIGITAL CONNECTIONS

AES or EBU: two channels of interleaved digital audio are sent through a three-pin XLR lead in a single direction. They are used by the professional industry and capable of long cable runs of up to 100 metres.

S/PDIF: popular with consumer and professionals alike, this protocol is transmitted through phono (RCA) leads or sometimes Toslink optical cables. Unlike AES or EBU, it has the capability of sending track indexing information and copy protection data. Minidisc and some computer soundcards also use optical leads.

ADAT optical: eight channels of digital audio available, transferred on optical cable to an ADAT machine that records onto VHS tape.

ADVANTAGES OF DIGITAL RECORDING

- Low noise
- Easily manipulated/processed
- Can be used by miniaturised equipment
- Can be sent via email or stored on servers; accessible globally
- Digital tagging capability for easy indexing and reference.

DISADVANTAGES OF DIGITAL RECORDING

- Some listeners describe digital recordings as cold
- Analogue allowed for its physical circuits to be overdriven to produce a warm, distorted sound; digital requires no hard-wired circuitry in the same way, so it does not facilitate the same type of sound manipulation
- Data must be archived when hard drives become full.

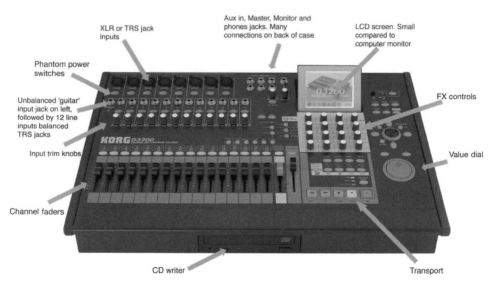

Korg D3200 Digital Multitracker

The studio environment

ROOM SETUP

If you are lucky enough to have a specialised room for recording your coursework, with a separate control room, then you will gain valuable experience from emulating professional practice. The control room houses the main computer or other hardware for recording; a mixer or audio production console, plus any outboard effects normally rack mounted; monitor speakers; and the cabling from the performance room, which is sometimes fed through a patch bay. Comfortable and supportive chairs are a must for long recording sessions and their soft furnishings also help with acoustics. The studio's amplifier might be sited outside, but in close proximity to the control room for reasons of noise and/or ventilation: in fact, anything that makes a noise should be sited elsewhere.

In a professional studio, the performance room will be visible through three sheets of angled glass to stop sound leakage. Recording environments for popular music benefit from a flat frequency response, avoiding an emphasis on reflected standing waves and unwanted bass boom. For popular music it is also desirable to be able to reduce reflections so that the room is relatively dead in acoustic terms. Reverberation is normally added artificially in this style of music and is therefore much more controllable. Carpets and acoustic tiling will help reduce the room's reverberation, and non-parallel walls and ceilings will cut out unwanted standing waves. There are various acoustic screens on the market that work well in absorbing higher frequency reflections. For lower frequencies, professional studios use bass traps. These are various boxes and frames designed to resonate with the low frequencies of the room, which need to be calculated before the units are designed. Windows are kept to a minimum, or at least covered to avoid the highly reflective hard glass surface.

The control room itself must also be considered from an acoustic point of view. If the monitoring sound has for example a high bass emphasis, which sounds great in the room, it is likely that the engineer will overcompensate and the recording will not have enough bass in the final mix down.

The engineer will want to monitor the sound that is being recorded or played back; a system of speakers and power amplifier will be in place. Sometimes powered monitor speakers are used, particularly for near-field monitoring. This method of monitoring is simple to use, avoiding any acoustic problems in the control room, although it can lack bass.

In the main performance room there will be a need for a number of balanced line inputs, hard wired and linked to the control room. Balanced lines use either a three-pin XLR connector or a TRS (tip, ring, sleeve) jack where two wires carry the signal and the third is used as a shield. This is useful for cutting out interference in long cables. The diagram below illustrates how two signal wires have opposite polarity and carry different information: the dark line and the light line are two different waveforms out of phase. Interference is picked up by both wires identically, so this unwanted noise is removed through phase cancellation – i.e. when added together they cancel each other out so no sound is heard.

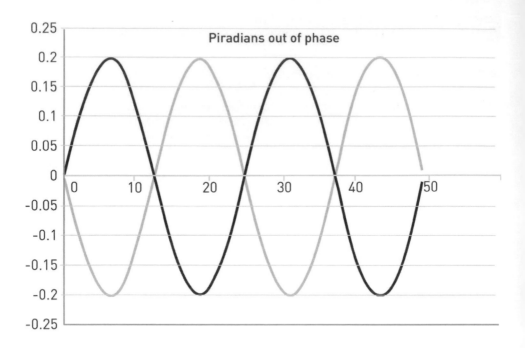

Piradians out of phase

There should be a stock of DI boxes (direct inject); active ones are better than the passive unpowered variety. Active DI boxes are quieter, have more facilities and can cope better with long cable runs. They need power, which can be either batteries or preferably the 48V phantom power sent from the mixing desk. DI boxes reduce high impedance guitar or keyboard outputs to microphone level, ready for input to the mixing desk. Also, it is convenient to find headphone distribution amplifiers so that musicians can easily maintain communication with the control room engineer and monitor any music. This would be done via a special cue mix sent from the control room (see page 19).

The performance room should avoid fluorescent lighting and other equipment that is likely to produce powerful magnetic fields, such as computers. It is very helpful if there are acoustic absorbent screens available to help with separation. Cable runs need to be as short as possible, with audio and power wires kept apart. Guitar players should be discouraged from using coiled jack leads; short straight leads will experience less interference. Separation from any external acoustic noise is also a consideration, and ideally the ring main will be separate from the main building, with a balanced AC supply.

If you do not have a separate control room then monitoring will have to be carried out with headphones. There are several factors to consider when using this approach:

- No signal from the left will reach the right ear and vice versa, unlike speakers
- Wearing headphones for a long time causes ear fatigue
- Ensure you wear closed headphones so that you get a truer idea of the sound going onto the recording, rather than the acoustic sound of the original

- An advantage will be that room acoustics do not affect the monitoring sound
- It is sometimes difficult to judge the stereo spread, with panned signals sounding less off-centre
- Make sure you wear headphones the right way round (left and right)!

The majority of modern studios run digital equipment and require very little outboard equipment, as the signal processing is carried out by software plug-ins. The signals are then fed to digital desks that completely interact with computer software and integrated systems such as Pro Tools. This makes the engineer's job a smoother process: fader automation and recall of previous sessions are the norm and there are very few problems with poor cabling.

Monitoring: amplifiers and speakers

SETTING UP A MIX

A studio engineer will need to set up a number of different mixes to listen to, as set out in the following table:

Name of mix	Who is it for?	Characteristics
Input mix	Engineer	A chance to check all inputs are functioning and at the intended level.
Cue mixes	Musicians	These sounds will not be recorded. They are produced to both enable the performers to follow the music for overdubs and to give them confidence. For example, a singer may like some reverb on their vocals but the sound will be recorded dry. A different cue mix might be sent to a different musician, so a drummer might not want the added reverb given to the vocalist. A cue mix is usually made with aux sends.
Monitoring mix	Producer/ engineer/ musicians	The sound that is monitored on the studio speakers. This of course may be sent to the musicians as well.
Recording mix (often the same or similar to the input mix)	Engineer	This is the sound that is sent to the recording machine. All tracks will be sent at maximum levels to ensure a good signal to noise ratio. A recording mix may perhaps be checked simply by visual means, i.e. careful observation of the meters.

A cue mix is set up using one or two of the auxiliary sends for each desired channel, together with a master send (which is assigned to a group and output). It is therefore important when purchasing a desk to ensure there are several auxiliary sends for each channel so that global effects can be controlled. If using a software recording package such as Logic or Cubase you will need to create an extra output bus and route it to different outputs on your audio interface if you want to produce a different mix for monitoring. Cubase has a special function for this called the control room mixer.

The sound in the control room will depend on the settings of the desk and any outboard effects, together with the power amp and the studio monitor speakers. These in turn are affected by any ambient reflections in the room itself. The musicians may be using a headphone distribution amp for their cue mix. The control room engineer will be feeding the monitoring mix to a power amp and studio monitors for the producer to listen to, or indeed the musicians or producer between takes.

AMPLIFIERS

Audio amplifiers take the low level power output of mixing desks, or electronic musical instruments, and bring it up to a level suitable for driving loudspeakers. The mechanical movement of the speaker cone and the diaphragm attached to it requires a considerable amount of electromagnetic energy; this is where the amplifier comes in. The original signal is not actually affected. However, it is copied and used to modulate (change) the power current of the amplifier itself – which has a much higher amplitude.

The power supply is key to the process. It does two jobs: first, it changes the power from alternating current to direct current; second, it ensures that this current is even and uninterrupted. The power output can then be modulated to match the shape of the input waveform. Battery powered amplifiers already use direct current.

Amplifiers will also include a pre-amplifier in their path so that the output can be boosted in stages.

Types of amplifiers are listed below:

Pre-amplifier	Part of the circuitry of an audio amplifier. However, they can also be separate units or built into a mixing desk or hardware digital recorder.
Power amplifier	This is the term generally used to describe the amp at the heart of a studio monitoring system. It would have very few controls on its fascia as the shaping of the sound would be carried out by the outboard effects units or on the mixing desk. Treble and bass controls would cause confusion.
Hi-fi amplifier	Domestic stereo systems would use an amplifier into which playback equipment is fed. It would feature an input select switch and treble, middle and bass controls with its own headphone output. This type of amplifier would not be found in recording studios.
Active speaker	Near field monitor speakers are often 'active' – i.e. they have an amplifier built in. One advantage of this system is that the speakers are perfectly matched to the built-in amps, unlike passive speakers that might be the wrong power or impedance. They usually feature adjustments for room acoustics on the back, together with output level, power-on sensors and balanced and unbalanced inputs.

Instrument amplifier	If used for practice or in the studio then these come with speakers built into the same unit and are known as combination or 'combo' amps. Guitar amps commonly feature a distortion option and a DI output for direct connection to a desk. Also spring reverbs are common along with other time-based effects. Compression is common in bass guitar amps.
	On stage the amp is likely to be separate from the speaker and is known as the 'head'.
	Unlike hi-fi and power amps – which are designed to reproduce the sound with minimum harmonic distortion or coloration – guitar amps often add their own sound to the instrument. So much so that favourite amps are nowadays modelled in software systems.
	Instrument amplifiers for acoustic instruments are designed to have a relatively flat frequency response and a clean sound. To achieve this they usually have high power ratings.
Valve/transistors	Vacuum tube or valve amps were the first portable models to appear in the 1930s with their built-in power supplies. In the 1970s, the cheaper and more convenient transistor amp was born. Many engineers prefer the warmer sound of the earlier tube amps and so these continue to be manufactured.

SPEAKERS

The amplified electrical signals reach the coil and magnet assembly in a speaker driver. This causes the cone that is attached (but flexibly suspended in the speaker basket or cradle) to move back and forth, copying the waveform that has been sent to it. This produces variations in air pressure that the human ear can detect.

A loudspeaker enclosure often includes different speaker drivers depending on the frequency range. These include:

- Woofers – the largest size designed to handle the bass frequencies
- Tweeters – small size for the upper frequencies
- Midrange – for the middle frequencies; less common than the two above.

The incoming signal needs to be broken up into the frequency bands required for the different drivers; a small electronic unit called a crossover does this job.

A crossover unit inside a speaker housing draws its power from the audio signal, i.e. it is passive and doesn't require external power. It employs electronic components called capacitors and inductors. Capacitors allow the high frequencies through so their signal is sent to the tweeter. Inductors allow the low frequencies through so they are linked to the woofer. Active crossovers exist but they are highly specialised and act before the signal reaches the amplifier.

Some speaker enclosures are not sealed. Instead, they have small openings called ports that allow the sounds produced behind the speaker cones to be redirected, to reinforce the vibrations from the front. One common type is known as a bass reflex speaker. Although these ported speakers use energy more efficiently, their sound is less precise than the enclosed versions.

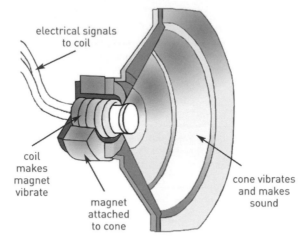

electrical signals
to coil

coil
makes
magnet
vibrate

magnet
attached
to cone

cone vibrates
and makes
sound

A diagram of a loudspeaker showing coil, magnet and cone

Other speaker technologies include electrostatic speakers that use large, thin diaphragm panels, and planar magnetic speakers that use a long metal ribbon suspended between two magnetic poles. The traditional dynamic loudspeaker is still by far the most common.

Microphones and microphone placement

Microphones are used to capture live sound for recording or sound reinforcement purposes. They can be used on balanced or unbalanced circuits (see page 17 and diagram on page 18). Balanced circuits are less prone to interference and are generally preferable. Unbalanced microphones can conveniently be used at line level and generally employ a cable ending with a standard jack lead.

The levels of electrical signals produced by microphones are very low, particularly with balanced lines, and will require a pre-amp to boost the signal to a useable line level. Pre-amps can be separate units or, more often, built in at the input stage of a mixer. The quality of your pre-amps will very much affect the quality of your recorded sound.

Microphones have various polar response patterns represented by the dark line on the following diagrams:

1. Omnidirectional:

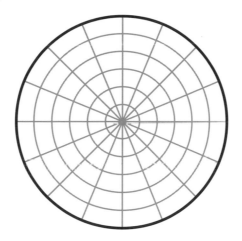

- picks up signals from all directions
- is sometimes used to capture a room acoustic
- is not used for sound reinforcement as it is likely to cause feedback
- has no bass boost when used close up (that is, no proximity effect)
- is not focused and picks up a general sound.

2. Unidirectional:

- is good at rejecting sounds from the rear, so it is used for separation between tracks
- is good at rejecting room acoustics and background noise
- has bass boost when used close up (called proximity effect)
- has various polar patterns:
  - cardioid, which has a broad angle pick-up in the front of the microphone, but very little pick up from behind

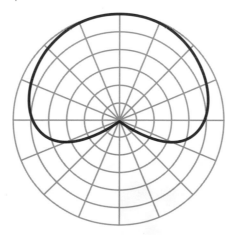

- supercardioid, which has more isolation than cardioid and is good for stage floor mic'ing
- hypercardioid, which has maximum side rejection, and is used for more focused front sensitivity.

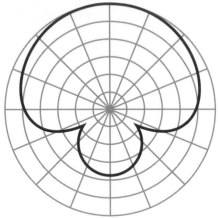

3. **Bidirectional (figure of eight):**

- picks up from front and back but not from the side
- can be used for backing singers, and overhead for an orchestral section
- often referred to as a figure of eight
- found in ribbon microphones.

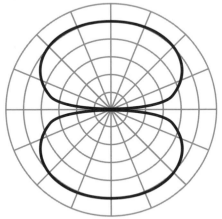

TYPES OF MICROPHONE

The function of a microphone is to convert mechanical energy via magnetism to electrical energy. There are a many different types of microphone, each with its particular application, as listed in this table:

Microphone	Description	Usage
Dynamic	■ Most straightforward and robust microphone on the market ■ Moving coil reacts to changes in sound pressure levels (SPLs) ■ SPLs are detected by a magnet; a fluctuating current is produced through electromagnetism ■ Cardioid polar response pattern ■ Can handle loud sounds well	■ Used particularly on stage for vocals ■ Used for amplification and recordings for guitar amplifiers
Condenser	■ Uses a low voltage for power and is very sensitive ■ Often has a low frequency cut-off (bass roll-off) switch, which reduces the proximity effect ■ More fragile than a dynamic microphone; it requires battery power or a low-voltage feed (phantom power, commonly +48V) from either a recording desk or a pre-amp ■ Can pick up a wide range of frequencies and is more sensitive than a dynamic to sounds at low volume	■ Preferred microphone for recording quiet sounds, particularly lead vocals where a large diaphragm version is used ■ Should be mounted in a shock-proof cradle to avoid picking up vibrations ■ Also used for the bright sounds of acoustic instruments ■ High-end models can be very expensive
Electret	■ The ferro-electric material used contains a permanent charge ■ A very small and affordable microphone	■ Mass produced and installed in computers, phones and other portable devices ■ Some high-end models used in studios
Piezoelectric/ PZM	■ Designed to be used on surfaces, such as on a wall or taped to the lid of a grand piano ■ Uses a mini condenser microphone mounted very near to a sound reflecting plate	■ Used as a boundary microphone ■ Good for room capture ■ Reduces phase cancellation
Stereo	■ Two directional microphone capsules in a single housing ■ Single-point recording cuts out phase shifting, and therefore recordings are highly mono-compatible (important for radio broadcasting, for example)	■ Useful as an approach to recording large groups ■ Convenient for portable recording devices

CLOSE MIC'ING

Placing microphones close to a sound source has the advantage of cutting out the sound of other instruments that might be in close proximity. This enables a clearer recording of the required source. However, recording at such close range means that sounds from an instrument's mechanics or a player's movements or breathing may be recorded unnecessarily. Close mic'ing has a very focused, tight and clear sound with little reverb.

If a nearby instrument is picked up in a close-mic recording it is known as spill. As well as moving unwanted sound sources away from the microphone, spill could be reduced by using an acoustic barrier – a self-supporting board covered in soft, absorbent material. (To avoid spill, unwanted sounds should be at a distance of five times the proximity between the microphone and the instrument being recorded.)

Some specialised microphones for brass and woodwind instruments clip on to the instrument (on the bell or near to the keys). There are sets of microphones designed to mic up a drum set, which include a kick-drum microphone that is responsive to bass frequencies and high SPLs; clip-on dynamics for snares and toms; and condenser microphones for overhead placement to capture the high frequencies of the cymbals.

AMBIENT MIC'ING

When recording in a space with a desirable acoustic – for example, a concert hall – microphones can be placed at a chosen distance away from the sound source, so that they capture the ambience of the room as well as the direct sound. Ambient mic'ing gives a sense of natural space to a recording. This mic'ing approach can be used in conjunction with close-mic'd techniques and then mixed together. When using several microphones, care must be taken to avoid phase cancellation; professional mixing desks will supply a polarity reversal switch at the top of an input channel to help avoid this problem (see diagram on page 18).

Stereo recording techniques often involve ambient mic'ing. There are a number of approaches to this:

- **A/B or spaced pair:** two microphones (usually omnidirectional) face the performers with a set distance between them. The recording engineer must ensure that the distance isn't too far as the result will produce mono incompatibility.

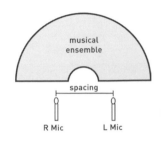

- **X/Y or coincident pair:** two identical directional microphones are placed with their heads as close together as possible (without touching) and facing inwards at 90 degrees. The microphone outputs are equally panned left and right. Sometimes a small space is introduced horizontally between the microphones (spaced pair), increasing its stereo feel but reducing its mono compatibility.

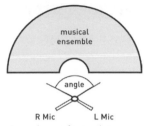

- **M/S (mid-side):** another coincident pair, but this time one microphone faces the sound source and picks up the direct signal (mid) while a second (bi-directional microphone) faces across and picks up the ambient reflections from the left and the right – with the two microphones often in one casing. The two signals are then mixed as shown in the illustration below. This method has two advantages: the reverberant mix can be altered after the recording has taken place, and there is a complete compatibility with a mono mix. This technique is often used in broadcasting and film.

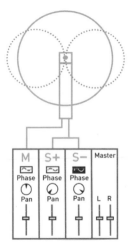

- **Baffled omni:** two omnidirectional microphones are set up with a baffle or dummy head between them. The advantage is that it offers a good bass response. The disadvantage is that it can lead to compatibility problems when mono recording is important.

For a discussion of the characteristics of stereo sound, see pages 61–2.

Mixing desks

Mixing desks have the following sub categories: mixer amps, audio recording consoles, live sound mixers, digital mixers and software mixers. These different types of equipment share the common design used by a basic analogue mixer. This type of mixer was commonly used in most recording studios, so it is the focus of this section. Other types of mixer are covered on page 32.

BASIC ANALOGUE MIXER

Mixers are described by the number of inputs they have, linked to the number of groups and the output. Therefore, a 24x8x2 would have 24 individual channel inputs, eight groups (or busses) and a stereo output. A bus (or buss) is a common electrical signal path along which signals may travel. These include the auxiliary, solo monitoring and main stereo busses. The word 'pot' is an abbreviation for potentiometer, which is a knob that adjusts a level upwards in a clockwise direction.

The desk will have one or more meters to visually indicate the input or output levels. These are either VU (volume unit) moving needles or coloured LEDs arranged as bar graphs, as shown in the illustrations below. Analogue meters do not reflect the true signal undulation but represent an average so that the needle can cope with the physical movement. (Some engineers prefer this to the rapidly moving bar-graph LEDs.)

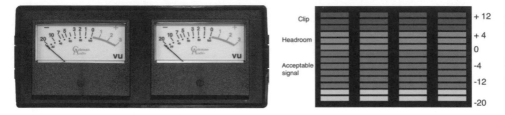

Solo and mute buttons will have an LED lit up when they are on. It is easier to use one solo button to hear a particular channel than muting all the other channels.

The illustration that follows represents the standard layout for a mixer. The input channels are arranged alongside each other with their common controls; these are known as channel strips. The functions of the various controls on the channel strips are explained in the table on pages 30–31.

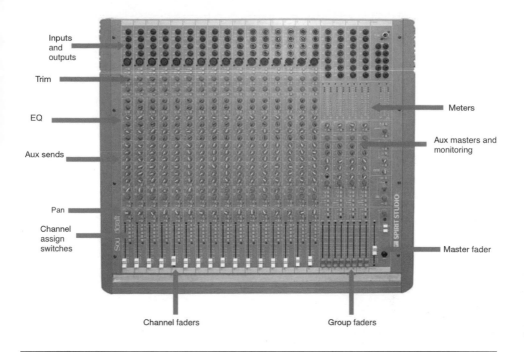

Inputs and outputs

Trim

EQ

Aux sends

Pan

Channel assign switches

Meters

Aux masters and monitoring

Master fader

Channel faders

Group faders

The layout of a mixer will vary depending on the manufacturer and model, the dedicated purpose of the mixer and its size. However, the description here covers the layout of the most common analogue consoles and mixers available.

When the fader moves above unity gain (0dB), every 6dB of boost results in a doubling of amplitude. Below should be marked as negative dB down to infinity (i.e. silence). The numbers are not distributed evenly but follow a logarithmic scale with the difference in their values getting larger.

On the right-hand side of the mixer (after all the channel strips) there will be more faders for the groups, with these assign buttons selecting where each group should be sent (most likely the master output, L/R).

It is important to remember to unassign your channels on the input strips from the L/R-out if you are sending to groups. Forgetting to unassign the channel will create a duplicate signal, which will not be affected by your alterations to the group.

A useful way of using group faders could be to assign all drums or perhaps backing vocals to a group output. This means that one fader can do the job of several.

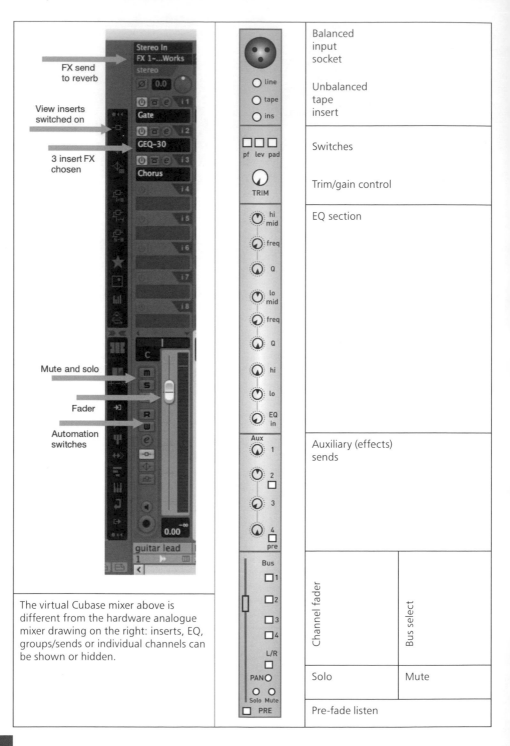

FX send
to reverb

View inserts
switched on

3 insert FX
chosen

Mute and solo

Fader

Automation
switches

Stereo In
FX 1–...Works
stereo
Ø 0.0
i 1
Gate
i 2
GEQ-30
i 3
Chorus
i 4
i 5
i 6
i 7
i 8

C
m
s
R
W
e

0.00

guitar lead
1

Balanced
input
socket

Unbalanced
tape
insert

Switches

Trim/gain control

EQ section

Auxiliary (effects)
sends

line
tape
ins

pf lev pad

TRIM

hi
mid

freq

Q

lo
mid

freq

Q

hi

lo

EQ
in

Aux
1

2

3

4
pre

Bus
1
2
3
4
L/R

PAN

Solo Mute
PRE

Channel fader	Bus select
Solo	Mute
Pre-fade listen	

The virtual Cubase mixer above is
different from the hardware analogue
mixer drawing on the right: inserts, EQ,
groups/sends or individual channels can
be shown or hidden.

XLR (cannon) connection for balanced lines, usually for connection to microphones.

Underneath is a balanced jack connection for line inputs. There is also usually a 'tape' input for playback and sometimes an insert point or direct out.

1. Phantom power – for sending 48V to power condensers and DI boxes.
2. Phase reversal switch.
3. Pad to reduce sensitivity of trim pot. Usually toggles between microphone and line ranges.

Trim adjusts the level of the input or gain.

In this diagram there are sweep EQs for four frequency ranges. In a modern mixer there is likely to be a greater provision, including parametric EQs and a switch to turn the EQ off and on for comparison of its effect.

The Q knobs govern the amount of spread around the selected centre frequency.

These govern the amount of the signal to be sent on the aux bus. No matter how much is sent, the original signal is not depleted. One common usage is to send a copy of the signal to an external effect. The aux master (a single knob that controls the output of all the aux sends) on the right-hand side of the desk needs to have a level – as does any return pot (or channel) that is governing the return from the effect unit. Pre/post-fader button available: the pre is useful for special mixes that do not want to be affected by the movements of the faders, such as for monitor mixes for musicians.

The channel fader will range logarithmically to make its effect more manageable. Three quarters of the way up (roughly where the fader is positioned in the diagram) is 0db or unity gain, where the signal is neither cut nor boosted.	Chooses where the signal is to be sent after leaving the channel. In this case it could be sent on either one of four groups or to the master output. Usually there is a pan option so that groups 1 and 2, or 3 and 4 can be blended.
Solo mutes all channels except this unless other solo buttons are pressed.	The Mute silences just this channel.

Enables the channel to be monitored ahead of the effect of the fader.

Above the group faders is the monitor section. Here you can choose what signals you send to the performance room speakers and/or headphones, control room speakers and headphones, and set their levels. There is sometimes a built-in electret microphone that you can activate by holding down a button. The electret microphone is used for talkback (communication with all the studio musicians), which will have its own send level pot.

Above the monitor section are the master pots, which control the levels of the aux send and solo busses. The effects return pots will also be here.

Above the master pots (at the top of the mixer on the right-hand side) will be the connections for the aux send and returns, groups and monitor outputs.

TYPES OF MIXERS

Mixers can be divided into recording and live mixers, analogue and digital mixers, powered and PA mixers, and software mixers (as part of a computer audio programme).

ANALOGUE MIXERS

Although digital technology became more affordable through the 1990s, digital mixers themselves remained relatively expensive. Therefore, it became common to find built-in digital effects in analogue mixers. Also fader automation became a feature of high-end mixers; a technology known as 'flying faders' and the ability to automate muting also became available (this was sometimes controlled by MIDI).

Mixers for live sound tend to be more simple. There is no need for tape-return inputs, for example, and they usually have fewer effects-sends but more monitor-outs, although obviously no controlroom output. There is no time for creative musing so simplicity is important, with portability and a rugged design to be considered. A PA amp with a number of inputs (controllable via individual pots) can be considered an analogue mixer.

DIGITAL MIXERS

These were first introduced in the 1990s but are now much more affordable. Control surfaces linked to computer software packages also come under this category: for example, the Control 24 linked to Pro Tools software with digidesign I/Os.

Advantages

- Easy recall of mixing sessions. This can even go as far as a session being saved on a memory stick by a mixing engineer and taken to a new venue with similar equipment. As far back as the 1980s some expensive analogue desks employed motorised flying faders for mix automation, but digital desks are far more capable in this area
- Full automation of all switches, faders and knobs
- Remote control via wireless laptop in live venue

- Built-in DSPs (digital signal processing) and the ability to use plug-ins developed by third parties
- Resistant to outside interference such as radio transmissions and mobile phone traffic.

Disadvantages

- Early models had severe latency problems, so much so that if two parallel paths used different processing, when recombined they would cause comb filtering effects. Latency was also very off-putting to artists trying to monitor their own performances in real-time. Powerful PCI cards and fast computer processors avoid this for control surface examples.
- The compact designs sometimes led to switches being assigned multiple tasks, which was off-putting for the novice user – particularly when quick adjustments needed to be made in a live situation.

VIRTUAL MIXERS

Virtual mixers are found in most of the mid-priced and more expensive music software. In Pro Tools there are two main pages that you can choose between: the mixer view and the track view, the second of which displays recorded tracks in a linear fashion with graphical representation of the waveforms.

Virtual mixers have all the capability of digital mixers without the hands-on aspect. They display (by default) all audio and MIDI tracks, with the outputs of any virtual instruments and effects returns together with any groups the user may have created.

One unique feature of virtual mixers is that you can customise your display. For example, channels can be viewed as wide or narrow; racks of effects can be hidden or revealed; channels can be named for easy identification. As with digital mixers, many controls can be automated – not just the fader movements but mutes and bypasses on-effects and rotating pan pots. The image that follows is a Cubase mixer in extended view. Note that channels can be set to display a number of parameters as shown at the top of the diagram. On the left there is a selection bar if all the channels need setting the same.

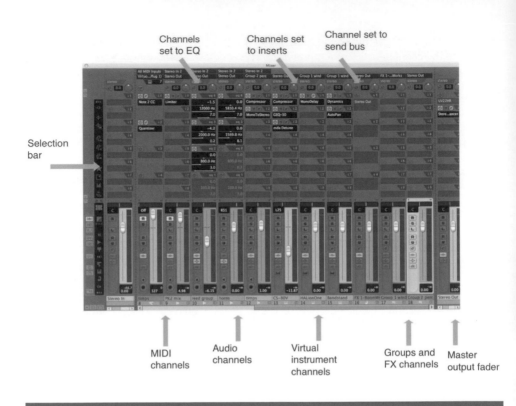

Channels set to EQ

Channels set to inserts

Channel set to send bus

Selection bar

MIDI channels

Audio channels

Virtual instrument channels

Groups and FX channels

Master output fader

Recording instruments and voices

ELECTRIC GUITAR

The most popular method of recording an electric guitar is to place a dynamic microphone (or a condenser with a pad switch to reduce the level) in front of the amplifier, just off the centre but not near the edge, about 15cm away. If placed near the edge then the sound will be lacking in the higher frequencies, which will result in a loss of brightness. Using a microphone in front of a speaker gives a full and immediate sound. However, it is important to avoid amplifier buzz or hum with the guitar acting as an aerial – this can be avoided by rotating the instrument to face another direction (or a noise gate can cut out unwanted sound at post production). To add presence to the sound a second microphone can be added, usually a condenser set about 5m away, depending on the room acoustics and the sound required. Also some amps have multiple speaker cones. In this instance, it is possible to use multiple microphones, choose the best sounding of the cones or back away slightly to capture a wider sound.

Some guitar amps have a DI (direct inject) output. For guitars that don't have this facility, a DI box can be used – preferably an active one (powered by phantom power or batteries) where a signal can be taken directly to the input of a mixing desk, as this will avoid any unwanted noise. Using a DI box gives a smoother, cleaner, but less immediate and unrealistic sound. To give the sound more edge, it is possible to use a processor designed to emulate the characteristics of a guitar amp. This method of recording, i.e. DI plus amp simulation, is particularly useful when recording with headphones. Amp modelling plug-ins can be found with most high-end digital recording software. The illustration that follows shows a guitar amp plug-in from Logic 9 software.

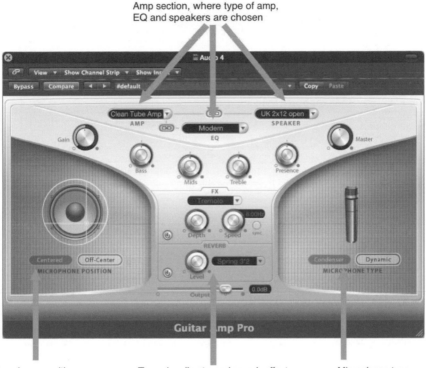

Amp section, where type of amp, EQ and speakers are chosen

Microphone position   Tremolo, vibrato and reverb effects   Microphone type

Combining recordings of mic'd-up amps and a DI'd sound to two tracks gives the best of both worlds. However, it is important to look at the phase characteristics of the waveforms in case of phase interference, particularly when recording a bass guitar.

More information on the function of the electric guitar can be found on page 76.

ACOUSTIC GUITAR

Condenser microphones are a must for recording acoustic instruments as they have a greater frequency range response. They are particularly effective when used with softer sounding instruments like the classical or finger-picked steel strung guitar. If possible use a large diaphragm vocal microphone positioned 50cm away (perhaps closer in a noisy environment) with its capsule pointing to the join between the neck and the body of the guitar. An alternative method of recording that captures a fuller range of tones from the instrument is to use two small condenser microphones: one pointing at the sound hole (about 30cm away), and one at the fretboard (around the 11th fret). A room microphone will add presence, depending on the acoustic. String lubricants can cut squeaking; generally, pick noise is not desirable, although this depends on the style of music.

BRASS AND WOODWIND

When recording wind instruments, it is possible to consider a wide variety of options – as summarised in the following table:

Instrument	Microphone	Technique
Trumpet/trombone	Dynamic	Place in the front of the bell, or slightly to the side for a more mellow sound.
Saxophone	Dynamic or condenser	Condenser for slight distance. Dynamic for spot mic'ing – be careful to avoid key-hole clatter. Supercardioid condenser clip-on microphones, with a wide dynamic range, are commercially available.
Flute/clarinet	Condenser	Sound emanates from the key holes and mouthpiece so a condenser placed above is best for recording.

PIANO

To capture faithfully the sound of a grand piano, ensure that the lid is up (or off completely) to avoid boom, and use condenser microphones to capture the brightness of the top strings. Try not to mic too close to the strings as you don't want just a few notes to be emphasised. About 30cm should be a good distance, with at least two microphones being used: one for the treble, one for the bass. If available, it is a good idea to tape a boundary microphone to the underside of the lid. Ideally, the condensers should use shock-mounts and be pointed towards the hammers; to avoid percussive noise, the condensers must be at least 20cm (horizontally) away from the hammers. An XY pair just outside the piano gives a more realistic and less close sound.

When recording an upright piano, try removing the front panel of the piano and mic'ing the strings with a pair of condensers (as customary with a grand piano). An alternative approach is to place the piano away from any nearby walls and mic the soundboard. The advantage of this option is that the microphones pick up less pedal thumps and other piano-action noises. Try to find the best-quality piano available to you, as recording techniques can't improve the instrument's original sound.

VOCALS

The best microphone for vocals is a large diaphragm condenser, placed in a shock-mount to avoid vibrations. Use a pop-shield to avoid the microphone emphasising the plosives.

> Plosives are the Bs and Ps of speech that produce a gust of air; when picked up by the microphone, these consonants turn into an unwanted pop.

If you don't have access to a pop-shield, you can make your own using a wire coat hanger and a pair of tights. When setting up the recording, it is also important to ensure that any sheet music isn't placed between the singer's mouth and the microphone. If using a music stand, put it directly behind the microphone and place it high up. This will cause the singer to look up, keep a good posture and sing straight into the mic.

DRUM KITS

It is valuable to use spot microphones for a drum kit. In modern recordings, the ability to adjust the tone qualities of the different drums and cymbals when mixing is crucial. However, it is not easy to avoid spill between one microphone and another. Therefore, careful preparation is the key; the microphone placement and choice of microphones is critical for a successful sound, as covered in the list below and the illustration that follows:

- Prepare your kit, ensuring any rattles from loose screws or squeaks from the kick drum pedal are removed. Tune and damp the drum heads, as it will be impossible to correct the pitches later. Remove the front drum head from the bass drum if you are recording popular music
- Use a specialist kick-drum microphone if you have one. These are dynamics designed for high SPLs. If you don't have a mini stand then you will have to angle a normal microphone stand inside the drum. Ensure that it is not too near the beater, otherwise the mic may pick up unwanted clicks
- Use clip-on dynamics for the toms. If you don't have these, position the microphones 5–8cm away from the skins at an angle of approximately 30 degrees
- Use a dynamic for the snare. An alternative to a dynamic mic is a condenser with its pad switch pressed to reduce sensitivity. Experiment with placing the microphone above and below the drum. Below emphasises the rattle of the snares; above will produce a rounder sound. You can use both and mix them, but you might need to reverse the phase of one to avoid frequencies being cancelled
- A small electret condenser is suitable for the high hat. It needs to be placed above the top cymbal, pointing down. If it were placed at the side of the high hat, the gust of air produced when the hats close would create unwanted noise
- The main cymbal sound and an overall mix of the kit is best captured with a pair of overhead condensers. The ride cymbal is frequently used for a more continuous sound than the crash, and mic'ing close to the raised bell at the centre enhances its characteristic sound
- Check the phase between all the microphones for phase cancellation (see page 17).

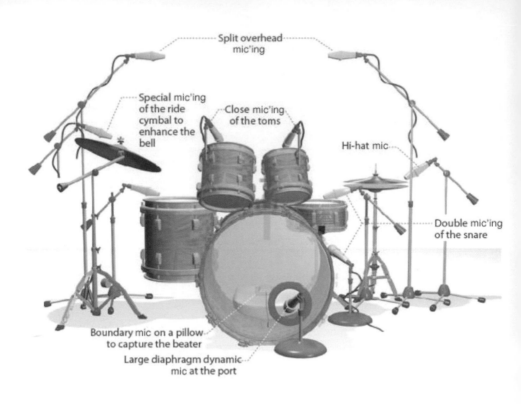

Split overhead
mic'ing

Special mic'ing
of the ride
cymbal to
enhance the
bell

Close mic'ing
of the toms

Hi-hat mic

Double mic'ing
of the snare

Boundary mic on a pillow
to capture the beater

Large diaphragm dynamic
mic at the port

MIDI and computer connections

MIDI is a system that allows different electronic musical instruments – such as synthesisers, drum machines, effects units, computers and even theatre lighting – to communicate with each other. MIDI stands for Musical Instrument Digital Interface. It is an 8-bit binary language that was standardised in 1983 enabling different manufacturers to link up their equipment. Each device would normally have a MIDI in, MIDI out and MIDI thru. The MIDI thru is used for connecting further devices in a chain, as this port sends an exact copy of what is present at the MIDI in port. The image below illustrates how MIDI can be employed between three synthesisers.

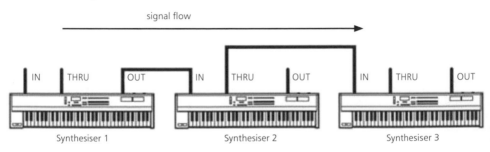

MIDI daisy chain distribution: note that it is now more common for MIDI devices to be connected via USB

SECTION 1: EQUIPMENT IN CONTEXT

The data transmitted via MIDI channel messages includes:

- Note-on and velocity (0–127)
- Note-off
- Channel aftertouch (key pressure only applicable to one channel)
- Program change – there are 128 (i.e 0–127) program preset sounds available as part of the General MIDI specification. They can be arranged in banks so that further sets of 128 sounds are theoretically possible (depending on the manufacturer)
- Control change includes modulation (CC1), main volume (CC7), pan (CC10), expression (CC11), sustain pedal (CC64) on and off, mono and poly modes (CC126, 127) as well as a number of synthesiser parameters
- Pitch bend.

As well as channel messages, MIDI employs system messages that are transmitted to all devices, which include:

- MIDI time code (MTC) – very useful for synchronisation and used, for example, to control lighting in time to music in stage shows
- Song position pointer
- Song select message – chooses between a number of different 'song' files stored on a sequencer or drum machine
- Tune request – sends an instruction to an analogue synthesiser to re-tune its internal oscillators
- End of message – signals the end of the system message.

System-exclusive messages are used to control a particular manufacturer's equipment. However, the General MIDI Standard first published by the MMA (MIDI Manufacturers Association) in 1991 defines a number of requirements for designers of synthesisers and sound modules to satisfy. This allows MIDI files to sound approximately the same when played back on different equipment.

The MMA specification includes:

- 24 note polyphony – i.e. at least 24 voices can sound simultaneously
- Keys must transmit velocity sensitive data
- 16 MIDI channels must be able to be used at the same time, with channel 10 reserved for percussion
- Multitimbral capability (different sounds at the same time)
- The arrangement of the 128 (0–127) programmed sounds must fit a particular order to ensure compatibility between playback devices and MIDI files. These are:
    - 1–8 keyboards
    - 9–16 chromatic percussion
    - 17–24 organs
    - 25–32 guitars
    - 33–40 basses
    - 41–48 strings and timpani

- 49–56 ensembles
- 57–64 brass
- 65–72 reeds
- 73–80 flutes
- 81–88 synth leads
- 89–96 synth pads
- 97–104 synth effects
- 105–112 ethnic
- 113–120 percussive
- 121–128 sound effects
- General MIDI 2 was released in 1999 and tried to bring together Yamaha's XG and Roland's GS developments. It included a further enhancement of patches together with some specific control message enhancements, which included filter resonance (CC71), envelope shapers (CC72, 73 and 75), vibrato (CC76–78), reverb and chorus
- General MIDI has a poor reputation among professional music producers, as the sounds themselves have become over familiar. It is still popular on the domestic front and for internet MIDI files.

Standard MIDI files come in three main formats:

- Format 0 – just one track, which (if the music has several sounds) will need to be de-mixed after importing to a sequencer
- Format 1 – with separate track information
- Format 2 – which contains song information, and is used by MIDI file players but not sequencers.

MIDI files are very small and there are a large number available for download on the internet. Their sound quality depends on a combination of how well the MIDI file was sequenced originally, together with the superiority of the sounds available on the playback device.

To connect a MIDI keyboard or sound module to a computer, it is necessary to have the right sockets. The Atari ST computer, available between 1985 and 1990 actually had built-in MIDI in and out which made it a favourite with musicians. Nowadays separate audio interfaces with MIDI connections built in have to be purchased.

Audio and MIDI computer interfaces

Originally, computers were developed for business use and so their sound capabilities were limited. In order to fill the gap in the market, the industry began to develop sound boards. These are extra circuit boards that are plugged in internally to a custom slot called a PCI, to provide a computer with the capability of recording and playing back audio and MIDI.

With the development of laptop computers, sound cards were manufactured for external use; these became known as audio interfaces or I/O devices (I/O stands for in/out). Audio interfaces used USB (universal serial bus) or FireWire systems to connect to computers. Also PCMCIA cards could be inserted into slots on laptops and connected to specialised MIDI/audio devices. The table that follows lists the standard data transfer rates currently available.

USB 1.1	USB 2.0	FireWire 400	FireWire 800	USB 3.0
12Mbps	480Mbps	400Mbps	800Mbps	5000Mbps (5Gbps)

Mbps stands for megabits per second. USB 1.1 is too slow for audio monitoring.

A good quality MIDI/audio interface is essential in today's modern studio. If the engineer or musician wants to hear playback of their music as they put it in (known as real-time monitoring), then the speed that the data is sent around the computer circuits is critical. This is called latency. Good quality audio drivers for Windows and Mac systems are now standard (the most well known being ASIO), making latency less of a problem. Latency was reduced in most recording software by adjusting the size of the audio buffers. However, there was a critical balance to achieve with the size of audio buffer: too small creates very little latency but horrible clicks and pops, as the computer operating system accesses the buffers too late and there is a resulting gap in the audio stream; too large creates a good sound but the latency is unacceptably long.

Sequencers and software

Among the most recognised sequencing packages on the market today are Logic (Mac only), Sonar (Windows only) and Cubase (Windows and Mac). They all use a virtual track environment and can manipulate both MIDI and audio with ease. (You will most likely have used one of these three software programs for your coursework.) Pro Tools software is a market leader in multitrack recording; it is used by the professional recording industry and it is very expensive to buy (although budget versions are now available). However, the strength of Pro Tools is audio; it does not have the extensive MIDI editing available as offered in Logic, Sonar and Cubase. The list that follows covers the core features offered by the three mainstream packages:

- A variety of MIDI editors, piano roll or graphic grid editors, score editors and detailed list editors
- The ability to adjust the timing of notes – when they begin and where they end (quantising)
- The ability to edit audio – actual audio recordings are stored unaltered in a separate folder and editing work is carried out in the sequencer's routines
- An audio/sample editor where detailed work can be carried out on the audio file
- A metronome to keep in time with when recording in real-time
- Time stretching and pitch shift

- Proprietary virtual plug-ins, both for software instruments and effects
- The ability to import third party plug-ins
- A virtual mixer that emulates the real thing, with sends, returns, faders, aux channels and effects racks
- The ability to automate faders, knobs and switches
- The ability to work with different sample rates and change them if necessary.

Signal processing

Audio signal processing refers to the intentional alteration or manipulation of the characteristics of a sound. It can be divided into a number of techniques, often referred to as effects, that cover areas such as the sound's tonal quality (for example, EQ or distortion), its dynamic properties, and its pitch or duration. Sometimes these alterations are applied over a time frame and regular changes are known as modulations.

EQUALISATION (EQ)

> The term equalisation derives from the early days of outside broadcasts by the BBC: long cable runs resulted in a reduction of the upper frequencies by the time the signal reached the recording van. The upper frequencies would be boosted to compensate – i.e. the sound would be 'equalised' back to its original.

Equalisation (EQ) is used for creative purposes, as well as increasing the clarity of the sound. Key facts to remember about the use of EQ are:

- A good rule of thumb is to cut rather than boost, as this avoids noise problems. For example, to achieve a brighter sound cut lower frequencies rather than boost upper ones, which avoids the noise problems that may occur through giving unwanted sound extra energy in the higher range of the audio spectrum.
- Moving the frequency control up and down with the gain set high can be used to search for a part of a sound (sweeping); when identified, the gain can be reduced to more useable levels
- EQ can be used to separate instruments in conjunction with panning
- Leave the EQ adjustments until late in your project. If you have worked extensively on the EQ of a particular instrument then the plug-in settings can be saved and recalled later at the mixing stage
- Boosting the middle frequencies too much can lead to a boxy sound
- Trust your ears more than your eyes and don't be tempted to overdo EQ – boosting all the top frequencies, for example. This can build up over a number of tracks and produce harsh sounds. Similarly too much cutting can lead to dullness.
- There are a number of EQ types: graphic EQ, fixed EQ, shelf EQ and parametric EQ. The details of these four EQs are covered below.

GRAPHIC EQ

This divides the frequency spectrum in a number of bands: not just treble, middle and bass, but ten, 15 or even 31 bands per channel. With 31, each band will cover $\frac{1}{3}$ of an octave. The many sliders for each band are moved up or down to boost or cut the relevant frequencies, resulting in graphic patterns. Graphic EQs are particularly useful for homing in on a particular noise, perhaps cutting a squeak from a kick-drum pedal or removing the sound of a fan-heater. This is called notch filtering. The term 'graphic' describes the fact that their normal usage will be to align all the sliders into a graphic shape. Therefore, for example, if the sliders rise and fall in a curve from left to right the result will be that middle frequencies are boosted. The illustration below is taken from the Cubase GEQ-30 Graphic.

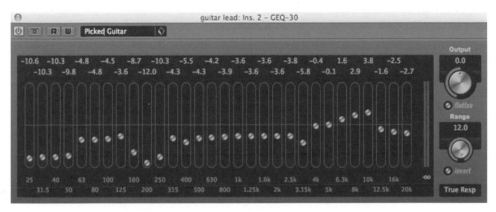

FIXED EQ

Commonly found on cheaper analogue mixing desks, this term refers to three band EQs concentrating on high, middle and low frequencies. Sometimes the mid range is divided into lo-mid and hi-mid to make four bands in total.

SHELF EQ

This applies a cut or boost to all frequencies that fall above (high shelving) or below (low shelving) the selected frequency. The diagram below shows the frequency response of a treble/bass EQ, using a low shelving filter. (Note: f stop is where the curve levels out; f turnover is at 3dB where the curve returns.)

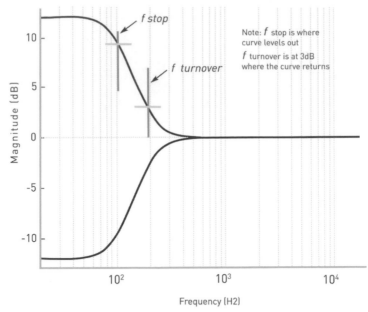

f stop

f turnover

Note: *f* stop is where curve levels out

f turnover is at 3dB where the curve returns

Magnitude (dB)

10

5

0

-5

-10

10^2 10^3 10^4

Frequency (H2)

PARAMETRIC EQ

A centre frequency is chosen and the signal is cut or boosted around it, the range of which is set by the Q control (sometimes known as the bandwidth control). The three controls are frequency, bandwidth and gain. First you select the frequency area you are working on; then you adjust the range of those frequencies, and then boost or cut them. It is common practice to boost a signal and then sweep the frequency pot slowly up or down to make the problem you are trying to sort out much worse. After you have arrived at the frequency, you change the boost to a cut.

In the diagram opposite the centre frequency is 10kHz. There are three bandwidths where the signal is being boosted, which would have been selected using the Q control.

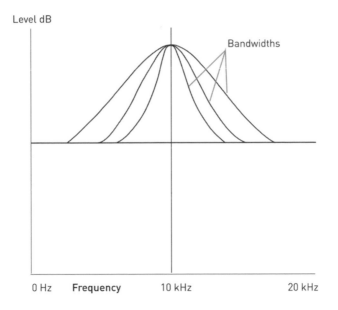

Level dB

Bandwidths

0 Hz   **Frequency**   10 kHz   20 kHz

The screenshot (below) from Propellerhead's Record shows a variety of EQ options. The mixing console features an EQ section with high and low pass filters, high and low shelving filters as well as parametric midrange filters.

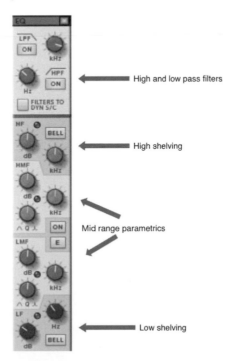

High and low pass filters

High shelving

Mid range parametrics

Low shelving

CONTROLLING DYNAMICS

Dynamics – in both a musical and audio-recording context – refer to the change in volume of a note. Sounds produced acoustically by the human voice or a musical instrument can employ a wider range of dynamics than can be effectively managed in electronically recorded audio. When the power output of a solo violin is compared to that of a forcefully struck orchestral bass drum, it is clear that the range cannot be adequately reproduced by speaker technology, either in the studio or the home environment. Furthermore, singers (for example) move around the microphone unevenly and so may not focus on the same area of the microphone's pick-up pattern, and guitar strings can often be plucked or picked in an uneven way. There are a number of processors available to the engineer to help with these recording and sound reinforcement problems.

The level of a sound is normally measured in decibels (dBs), which is based on a logarithmic scale: 0dB is the lower threshold of human hearing; 140dB is the sound of a jet engine at a range of 30 metres away. The range from minus infinity to +10dB can commonly be seen as a printed calibration on the channel strips of most hardware mixers: 0dB is a setting in a mixing desk where the sound passes through unaffected; anything above increases its level; a negative value will attenuate (reduce) it.

Control of dynamics is therefore a vital part of the recording, mixing and mastering process. The tools at an engineer's disposal include compressors, limiters, noise gates, de-essing, ducking and fader control, the settings of which can all be automated.

COMPRESSION AND LIMITING

Every audio system compresses the sound to a certain extent. There is an energy loss involved when the signal changes from one medium to another: from acoustic sound to magnetic and electrical energy and back again. Furthermore, the resistance of electrical circuits and mechanical linkages reduce the dynamic range. Loss of gain is rectified by amplification but there is a compression of the waveform nevertheless.

Even the human ear uses automatic compression of sound. The mechanical linkages, and the muscle that controls them, can serve as a safety against dangerously loud levels over short periods – although it is not very fast reacting. It can also help with the perception of extremely quiet sounds.

The historical development of dynamic compression can be summarised as follows:

- The world's first dynamic compressor was the Telefunken U3; built in the 1930s and used in the 1936 Olympic Games
- Military research contributed to the development of compressor technology
- In the 1940s and '50s compressors and limiters were used as overload protection devices in radio broadcasts
- Compressors and limiters were frequently built into amplifiers especially for instruments such as the bass guitar, to avoid overloading the speakers

- In early broadcasting, levelling amplifiers were used to match the recorded levels of different programmes
- A particularly well-thought-of valve tube compressor was the Rein Narma Fairchild 670 invented in 1959; noted for its smooth, warm sound
- In the middle of the 1960s, market leaders included the Teletronix LA-2A and later the Urei 1176; both were very effective on vocals, but were also commonly used for drums and bass
- Nowadays many of the vintage compressors have been reborn as software plug-ins
- The use of compression has changed over the years. In the 1960s, for example, compression was used to keep dynamic levels under control. Today it is used more creatively, for example forcing extra rhythm in dance music.

A compressor is an automatic fader that reacts to sounds above a given level and reduces them by a set amount. Acoustic sounds frequently contain peaks or short spikes of unwanted higher-level sounds that will determine the maximum SPL (sound pressure level) before distortion occurs. If these peaks can be reduced, the whole recording level can be set higher – thus raising the quieter parts of the sound's audibility. If applied at the mixing stage, then this instrument or voice track is less likely to disappear under other instruments and its presence is improved.

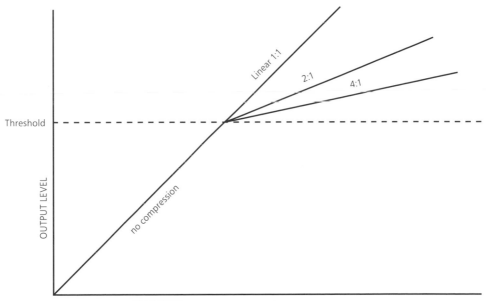

There are a number of common controls for all compressors:

- Threshold – this setting determines the level the sound should have reached before compression is applied; sounds above the threshold are compressed and sounds below are left unaffected

- Ratio – when the sound level crosses the threshold, compression is applied at a settable ratio. For example, 3:1 means that the input signal has to increase by 3dB for the output to increase by 1dB; 15:1 therefore reduces the output even more dramatically; 1:1 means no compression is applied.
- Knee – a hard knee means that compression is immediately introduced at the threshold; a soft knee means the process begins just before the threshold and reaches the set level just after (applying the effect more gradually). The graph below illustrates this. A soft knee is less noticeable to the human ear and so the result can sound more natural.

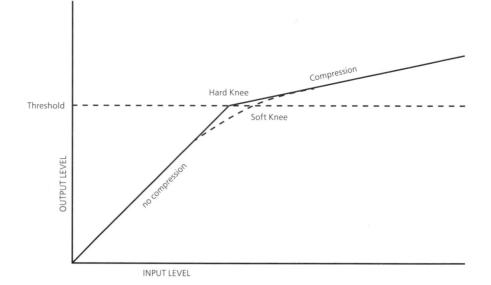

- Attack time – this refers to how long it takes to apply compression after the sound has passed above the threshold
- Release time – how long it takes for compression to cease after the sound has dropped below the threshold.

> Note: the human ear can pick up a sudden change in dynamics. By using a slightly more gradual attack/release, the effect can be more subtle when the dynamic change comes in.

- Input gain – adjusts the level of input to the compressor; this is important for avoiding distortion
- Output gain – this is sometimes called make-up gain. After the compressor has done its work, the overall level of the sound will be reduced and the opportunity to bring up the level to its previous power (without the peaks and the quieter sounds boosted) is now available. The amount of gain reduction can be observed with a meter display
- A bypass switch – this turns the effect off and enables quick comparisons to be made
- Stereo link – this links two mono compressors; it is particularly useful if the same settings are required for L and R channels otherwise the stereo image could drift around

■ Side chain input – is used for accepting external signals, other than the main input for controlling ducking and de-essing (see section on page 52). A copy of the input signal is fed to a side chain, which is monitored by the compressor. It is possible to filter the tone so that the processor is more or less sensitive to different frequencies

■ Peak/RMS – peak mode is for catching fast, transient peaks and is more accurate than the levelling mode of RMS, which is based on averaging.

> Some units can divide the frequency spectrum into bands. Different compression settings can be applied to each band; this is known as multiband compression.

Threshold and ratio controls work together. Although a low threshold would give more compression to the sound, if a moderate 3:1 ratio is used a subtle level reduction across the sound will be produced. A more aggressive result would be produced by a high threshold setting with a heavier compression 10:1 to capture the few rogue peaks. It very much depends of the nature of the original recording, with a ballad singer likely to require different compression settings to a hard rock rhythm guitar.

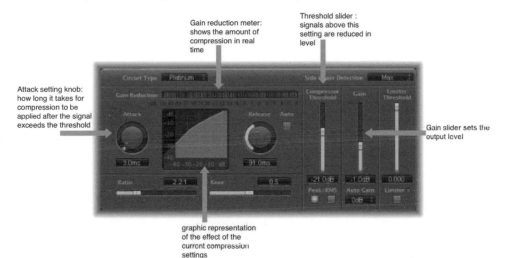

Gain reduction meter: shows the amount of compression in real time

Threshold slider : signals above this setting are reduced in level

Attack setting knob: how long it takes for compression to be applied after the signal exceeds the threshold

Gain slider sets the output level

graphic representation of the effect of the current compression settings

Compressor plug-in from Logic Express 9

LIMITING

A limiter is a type of compressor that uses a hard-knee change at the threshold with fast attack and decay times. A very heavy compression ratio that lets very little of the sound rise above the threshold setting is used, such as 20:1 or above.

Sometimes a limiter is used together with a compressor (the previous illustration shows how the two are combined into a single processor). When used together, the limiter is usually set to just clip out the loudest peaks.

Limiters can be applied to the entire mix output to prevent clipping, especially when the music is in a hard, driving rock, electronic or dance style. Overuse in other music can lead to the a rather dead sound. A limiter can also be used as a safety measure to prevent damage to PA equipment.

NOISE GATES

A gate performs just as its name suggests: it is either open to let a signal through, or closed to keep it from sounding at all (or significantly reducing it) – depending where the engineer sets the threshold.

A noise gate is traditionally used when recording with a microphone so that unwanted background sounds (such as amplifier hum) can be minimised. No sound is recorded when the player is resting, as the gate is closed because the noise does not exceed the threshold. However when a musician produces sound, the level is high enough to open the gate and any offensive noise is drowned out.

Noise gates can be used to help separate instruments: for example, recording a top tom part on a drum kit where there may be leakage from the snare, although it could prove difficult to set the threshold for a player using a range of dynamics. In addition, they are frequently used in live performance where intrusion from stage lights or other electronic equipment might cause interference.

As well as controls for threshold, attack and decay, noise gates sometimes feature a hold time. This keeps the gate open a little longer to ensure the decay portion of the sound is not cut off prematurely if it falls below the threshold. Also, a range control can reduce the sound level below the threshold rather than cut it off completely, to create a more natural sound.

In the diagram below the low level sound at the start is substantially reduced, but when its output level crosses the set threshold the gate opens (not instantaneously as the attack time softens this). When the output levels drop the gate closes and the sound output is reduced to a very low level (with the hold and release times softening the impact). The attack, hold and release times help to make the effect less noticeable and more natural to the human ear.

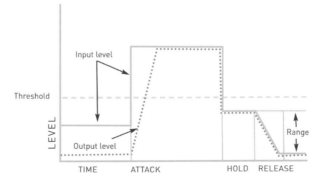

SECTION 1: EQUIPMENT IN CONTEXT

In a modern recording studio, digital equipment is less affected by unwanted sounds than in the days of analogue tape recorders. Digital equipment is inherently less noisy. Digital desks and high-end recording software can use automation to mute channels that have open (turned on) dormant microphones, but sometimes it is simpler to apply noise gates to these channels. Applying a gate to the complete mix is less useful as there is a risk of cutting quiet sounds that are needed to create the natural acoustic.

Noise gates are also used in more creative ways, often by being imaginative with the side chain input. One example of this is using one instrument to trigger another – a kick-drum signal fed into the side chain could be used to trigger a snare, forcing the instruments to synchronise. The gate applied to the snare drum sound would only open when it receives a substantial signal from the kick drum plugged into the side chain input.

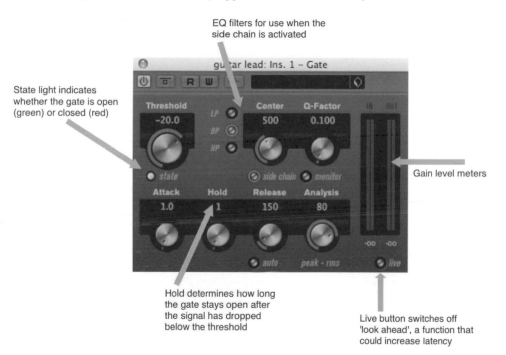

EQ filters for use when the side chain is activated

State light indicates whether the gate is open (green) or closed (red)

Gain level meters

Hold determines how long the gate stays open after the signal has dropped below the threshold

Live button switches off 'look ahead', a function that could increase latency

EXPANDER

An expander reduces the output level for signals below the set threshold. An expander's ratios are the opposite of a compressor so 4:1 will turn out to be 1:4. For every 1dB increase in input level there will be a 4dB increase in output. However, this is taking place below the threshold. The result is an increase in dynamic range, although accompanied by an overall quieter level; expanders are generally used to make quiet sounds even quieter.

DE-ESSING

This is a processor that is used to remove the harsh sounds of sibilants, i.e. 'sh', 'ss' and so on from vocals. De-essing uses a combination of EQ and compression. The sound is split into two channels. Sounds between 5kHz and 10kHz are enhanced by the EQs; the sounds in this range are then fed to the side-chain input of the compressor causing it to be more sensitive to these frequencies. The volume of these frequencies is then automatically reduced by the compressor when the vocalist produces them.

DUCKING

This is another compression-based effect very much employed by DJs and radio presenters. The volume of one channel is reduced when a signal is present on another channel, therefore music can be reduced in level when the spoken word needs to dominate. The presenter's speech will be fed into a compressor's side-chain input, and equipment should be set using a fast attack time to immediately reduce the music but with a longer release time so the music returns to normal less abruptly. Ducking is also used in music, notably when a guitar part becomes the accompaniment to a vocal and needs to be slightly reduced in volume.

DISTORTION

It was common in the days of analogue recording to turn levels up high to drive the system to its full capacity. Distortion normally is an unwanted change of the signal produced because the circuitry is overdriven. Guitar players soon found that over-driving their amplifiers produced a sound that was not just less defined but was also thicker and warmer. Digital equipment doesn't respond in the same way to high-level signals producing unwanted crackles and clipping.

Distortion as a useable effect is therefore often generated by analogue foot pedals or amplifiers. The three main types of distortion effects are overdrive, distortion and fuzz; the first being generally milder and the last more pronounced.

TIME-BASED PROCESSING

DELAY

The simple echoes produced by a delay unit were first created by tape systems, to utilise the difference in placement between the record and the playback head. A loop of magnetic tape would pass the record head where the signal would be imprinted. After a short time, the loop would then pass the playback head (or a number of spaced playback heads). The output of the playback head could be adjusted; the speed of the circulating tape could also be altered, and so there was a considerable amount of variation available in the output of the sound. One drawback was tape wear; artists would carry a stock of replacement loops with them. One ubiquitous model was the WEM copycat that dates from 1959, pictured opposite.

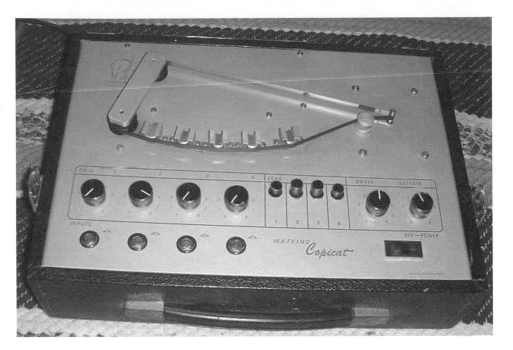

Not all delay units used tape. The Binson Echorec employed a revolving magnet drum and so was well known for its durability. (It was famously used by Pink Floyd.)

Tape-loop machines, with multiple playback heads and variable speeds, were used from the 1950s to the '70s to produce echo effects. Analogue non-tape delay effects came on the market in the 1970s and were based on a 'bucket-brigade' series of capacitors; they were used particularly in guitar pedals. These created a warm series of reducing echoes but couldn't produce long delay times.

Electronic versions of these tape-loop machines made matters easier – although at first the time a sound could be held back was quite short. As digital delays appeared and memory chips became cheaper, sound could be momentarily held for longer and longer times.

Delaying a signal for a set time and then playing it back can have a number of applications in both recording and live performance. A delayed signal can be fed back into the processor a number of times (feedback) to produce multiple repeats of the original; stereo (or dual mono) delays can handle signals differently.

The table following lists the common types of delay:

Delay type	Characteristics
Mono delay	■ Basic controls of delay time and feedback ■ Commonly found in guitar pedals
L/R stereo delay	■ Two mono delays, with separate controls: setting slightly different times on each control produces a rich sound
Multitap delay	■ A number of different delay times can be set, with each tap being a single delay line
Doubling echo/ ADT (automatic double tracking)	■ Very short delay times (20–40ms) produce the effect of double tracking, which creates the impression of two performers; this is useful for thickening the texture ■ Sometimes a slight pitch-shift is applied to the copied part, together with a small amount of panning ■ Famously used by John Lennon in 1966
Slapback echo	■ Delay time of between 100–200ms with little or no feedback of the delayed signal, which can emulate some hard-walled rooms ■ Common in 1950s rock and roll ■ Notably applied to vocals in the days of Elvis and Sun records
Ping-pong delay	■ The echoes are fed alternately to left and right channels
Straight delay	■ Delay lines are sometimes employed in large venues, which have speakers installed at the front and back, to help make up for the difference it takes for the sound to travel to the listener sitting at the back, away from the sound-source
Tempo delay	■ This sets the delay time to match the tempo of the music, so, for example, a single crotchet note might have three more semiquaver repeats, each reducing in volume. Famous use of tempo delay can be heard in Brian May's guitar solo in 'Brighton Rock' (from Queen's album *Sheer Heart Attack*, 1973) where the music builds into an ever expanding harmonic texture.

CHORUS

This effect uses frequency modulation (vibrato) produced by an LFO (low frequency oscillator), combined with a small delay, to produce the sound of a number of performers (i.e. a chorus). The controls available are:

■ Depth – sets the amount of pitch shifting of the LFO
■ Rate – sets the speed at which the LFO works
■ Mix – how much of the effect is applied to the original signal
■ Sync – software plug-ins can set the LFO to match the speed of the music.

Large amounts of chorus can produce sci-fi sounds; small amounts produce a subtle warmth. This sound effect is commonly heard on 1960s and '70s vocals. On the next page is the chorus plug-in from Cubase software with a preset setting for a crunchy guitar sound.

Width is the setting for the depth or amount of pitchshifting of the LFO

Mix: how much chorus is applied to the original signal

Rate: speed of the LFO

Sync button: to match the speed of the LFO to the music

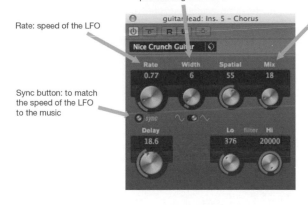

FLANGING

The effect of flanging is produced when a sound is delayed and the delay time is modulated (with the signal then fed back to the input); it creates a strange metallic sound. The effect takes its name from its original method of production using tape reels. In reality, two identical signals are mixed together; one of them has a varying delay time, which results in a comb filter that sweeps up and down the frequency spectrum. A feedback loop enhances this resonant effect. Popular in the late 1960s and through the 1970s, the effect has now fallen out of favour through overuse. Below is the Cubase flanger plug-in using a preset suitable for strings.

Feedback controls the character of the flanger effect – higher settings produce a more metallic sound

Sweep rate set freely when sync is off

Sync button keeps flanger sweep in time with music

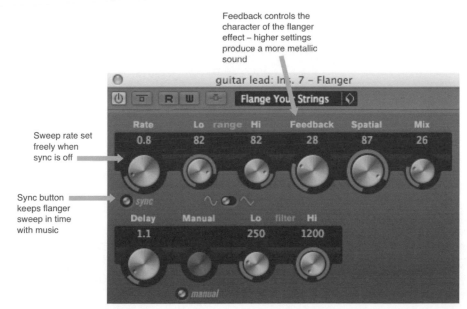

PHASING

If a phaser effect is applied to a sound, the tonal character of the sound changes through varying the interaction between two signals. This can produce interesting swirling sounds. The process can be controlled by an LFO and is more effective if applied to harmonically rich sounds such as strings or synth pads. Below is the Cubase phase plug-in using a preset swirling effect.

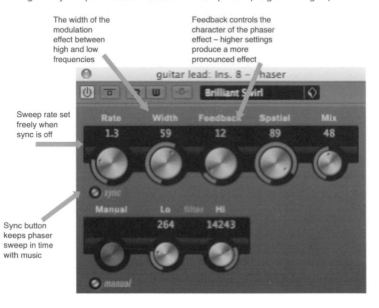

Because chorus, flanging and phasing are all time-based effects involving modulation they can sound rather similar and are used in similar ways in recording or performance. They make the music richer and more interesting but because they are artificial they should be used sparingly if a natural sound is required.

WAH-WAH

Wah-wah is a pedal controlled band-pass filter that sweeps up and down the frequency spectrum of a sound to create a spectral glide. This effect is commonly found in guitar pedals. It is used frequently in funk music and is supposed to imitate the opening and closing of a trumpet mute.

REVERBERATION

Although simple delay can be used to create a sense of space it is a little basic on its own. Reverberation is more effective because it uses multiple delays – complex echoes that can mimic the natural reflections of sound produced in an enclosed space, whether a cathedral, cave or concert hall.

The first type of reverberation to be used in recording was the use of natural spaces and careful microphone positioning. Natural reverb can be captured from an enclosed space, by creating a distance between the sound-source and the microphone placement reflections. The room acoustics will therefore determine the nature of the reverb. Omnidirectional and boundary microphones will pick up a greater number of reflections than unidirectional mics.

Some studios had special hard-walled rooms (often underground or in a basement) called echo chambers. In these spaces, a sound was sent from the control room and played over a speaker. Then a microphone at the far end of the room would capture the sound and the reverberated sound would be sent back to the control room. This reverberation of course could only be edited by changing the microphone position, adding in absorbent materials or by mixing different amounts with the original signal.

Spring reverb was first encountered in a Hammond organ in the 1930s. The soft furnishings to be found in the living rooms of the American public absorbed any sound reflections; if the instrument was going to have any chance of imitating a church organ, reverberation had to be added artificially. The long length of the spring was accommodated in the separate 'tone cabinet' that held the speakers. Later however the desire for smaller, self-contained organs necessitated the design of a shorter length spring reverb. Hammond engineers invented the 'necklace' reverb, which used several springs taking up just over a square foot in space. One problem this created was that the springs used to bang against each other and against their metal frame, creating an offensive crashing sound. In the 1960s Hammond developed a more effective unit called a type 4, which was used by many other manufacturers in their products, including the famous guitar amp produced in 1952 known as the Fender Twin Reverb.

Spring reverb uses a long spring to pass the signal through. It characteristically produces a mid-range boost with a long reverb time. It became common to have spring reverbs built into combo amplifiers. The sound was very effective, if a little metallic; it suffered the same problem of creating noise if the amp was knocked.

One particularly successful reverb of this type was known as The Great British Spring (1981). It was suspended in a plastic tube about a metre long and usually wall mounted: it produced a bright transparent sound, but would become harsh when overdriven.

The EMT-140 **plate reverb** was released in 1957, which rapidly became an industry standard and is still used today in studios and in software emulations. It employed a large thin metal sheet suspended in each corner of a wooden case with a centrally mounted transducer to generate vibrations. These were then picked up by a microphone-style pick-up transducer placed on the edge of the plate. The RT60 of the reverb was controlled by an adjustable damping pad combined with the send control. The warm dense sound produced was particularly suited to vocals and drums.

> RT60 is used to calculate reverb time; it is measured to the end of when the signal has reached -60dB – i.e the sound is effectively inaudible.

The same German company, EMT, was responsible for the first commercial digital reverb in 1976. This was named the EMT-250. Although it produced an excellent sound, it was rather expensive.

In 1978, the Lexicon 224 was unveiled, which became the most popular high-end digital reverb unit in history. It possessed interchangeable programs to simulate chambers plates and rooms.

In 1985, Roland produced their SRV-2000 digital rack mountable reverb unit with MIDI. It became extremely popular, as it produced a realistic sound and possessed large numbers of settings at an affordable price.

Originally produced as stand-alone units, digital reverb is now frequently to be found as a software plug-in as part of a sequencing package. Modern computer systems can generate a variety of reverb patterns using algorithms that simulate the traditional analogue systems or imitate different environments. Common controls for these include:

- Pre-delay – a gap between the sound and the application of the reverberation
- Reverb time – the time it takes for the reverberations to fade back to -60dB
- Size – refers to the imaginary size of the room that is being simulated
- Early reflections – this is the bounce-back from imaginary objects that might take place before the main reverb; it can give the processed sound more bite
- Density – how complex the reflections are (for example, those from an uneven wall are likely to be scattered in all directions)
- High and low frequency controls – these are available to adjust the tone to match the absorbency of varying environments; some spaces produce a brighter sound than others depending on the hardness of the walls
- High frequency damping – increases the warmth of a space by simulating how soft furnishing would absorb the high frequency reflections of a room
- Presets – are commonly found on digital reverbs, as are plug-ins, which often have delay settings. Environments and equipment that can be emulated include halls, chambers, rooms and spring/plate reverbs.

Opposite is Avid Audio Pro Tools's famous D-verb reverberation plug-in showing its preset programs and level sliders.

Diffusion – sets the degree to which initial echo density increases over time

Pre-delay – sets the amount of time which elapses between the input of a signal and the onset of reverberation

Preset programs

Decay – controls the rate at which the reverb decays after the original direct signal stops. Unusual use of the term 'decay' to refer to reverb time

The Sony company produced the first **convolution reverb** hardware unit in 1999 (DRE-S777), which used acoustic samples from real spaces such as halls and churches (stored on CD-Rom). In this process, an impulse signal (a short loud sound such as a gunshot) is played in the room first and the resulting reverberation is digitally recorded. Later the impulse signal is removed and the reverberation added to the required sound in the mix.

The first convolution reverb plug-in was invented in 2001 and was called altiverb. This also used sample technology rather than the algorithms of digital reverb.

PITCH SHIFTING AND TIME STRETCHING

Digital technology makes it possible to alter the pitch of music without it speeding up. This is very useful, for example, if a singer wants the backing track transposed down so they can easily reach the high notes. Similarly, the engineer can make music last a longer or shorter time without it becoming lower or higher in pitch. This of course is ideal for use in film, where it is imperative to match the music cue with the on-screen visuals. With pitch shifting and time stretching there are a number of factors to consider:

- Too great a change in pitch will result in the music sounding strange – squeaky if raised too high and sounding dark and subterranean if lowered. It is best to use small increments of a semitone or tone at the most.
- A time-stretching processor adjusts the length of a part by skipping or repeating individual samples; this can result in long time stretches sounding echoey and metallic.
- If possible, try cutting audio into sections before using time stretching; this will help to retain a more natural sound.
- One specialist device that uses pitch shifting for musical purposes is called a harmoniser. This will shift the note to a preset musical interval and play it back, together with the original, to create parallel harmonies. Programmes allow the fixed interval to vary according to key.

■ Auto-tune plug-ins have become popular in the last decade. These monitor a singer's vocal line and move pitches either to the closest semitone or a chosen scale or selection of notes, to help keep them in tune. They are more correctly called 'pitch correctors' rather than 'pitch shifters'. The note-to-note steps that result can sometimes be deliberately overused for special robotic effects, e.g. Cher's performance of 'Believe' (1998) is a pioneering example.

APPLYING DIGITAL SIGNAL PROCESSORS

When using audio plug-ins with computer software it is a good idea to remember the following points:

■ Real-time application – a set of instructions is applied while the original file remains unaffected. If used in moderation the load on the CPU is relatively light. This can then concentrate on maintaining playback timing accuracy.
■ Non real-time – an effect is selected and tested. When the user is satisfied the file is frozen, or locked. What has actually happened is a new file has been created with the effect embedded. This is what is played back.
■ A good way to reduce the load on the CPU created by heavy processing is to use a single instance of an effect and send a different amount from each track via a specially created path, which is then returned to the main output. These pathways are known as effects-sends and effects-return busses; they are preferable to using individual inserts particularly for time-based effects. Dynamic-based effects, such as compression, are better if used on individual inserts as they do not require mixing with the original signal.

Mastering

This is the process of preparing your recording for burning to CD, or another finished format. It assumes that you have a final mix you are happy with and then applies some careful compression, EQ and limiting across the stereo output to maximise the overall level. Some engineers favour a light stereo enhancement applied to the high frequencies to help widen the stereo spread, but this depends on the type of music. Preserving the dynamic range is a consideration when mastering classical CDs.

The beginning and the end of the track needs to be trimmed to ensure a clean product, with any unwanted noise removed. If the audio has been recorded at a high bit-depth (for example 24-bit professional quality), it will need to be reduced to 16 bit to match the CD standard with a 44.1kHz sample rate. In order to carry this out with a minimum loss of quality, dither has to be applied – there are customised plug-ins available to carry this out, such as apogee.

> Dither is the introduction of small amounts of unobtrusive randomly generated noise into the conversion process.

Commercial mastering houses have a reputation for creating a certain sound, or sonic character, and artists use these on a regular basis. In today's world, the original recording and the following mixing might have taken place in a number of locations and over a period of time; it might take a specialist to bring it all together.

Stereo and surround sound

Stereo sound is not just two signals – that is known as dual mono. True stereo gives a sense of depth to a sound in a similar way to stereoscopic pictures. The brain takes the two signals and works out – by comparing the timing differences of the various frequencies – how far away or how near a sound is sourced, imparting to it a sense of presence.

- 1881 – The phenomenon was first demonstrated to the public in Paris where a performance at the opera was relayed to a remote suite of rooms where listeners could experience it through twin telephone receivers.
- 1900s – In England, licensed users at home (or passers-by in hotels and cafés, where coin operated equipment was available) could pick up transmissions with an electrophone. These transmissions used telephone systems and the headsets were known as binaural. However, the telephone entertainment system was doomed to failure as a national radio network emerged.
- 1925 – The BBC broadcast an experimental AM stereo programme, which required the radio to have two tuners; FM radio (which was in stereo) didn't arrive until 1961.
- 1932 – A recording of the Russian composer Scriabin's *Prometheus: Poem of Fire* was made by the conductor Leopold Stokowski and the Philadelphia Orchestra; it was the first known stereo recording. The recording was created by twin styluses cutting two grooves into a wax disc.
- 1933 – Alan Blumlein at EMI made the real breakthrough in stereo recording when he patented stereo record technology; he also invented methods of stereo sound for film and even early surround sound techniques.
- Mid 1950s – EMI was recording on stereo tape; by the end of the decade vinyl stereo LPs were being commercially produced. The technology involved combining vertical and lateral movement of a stylus. Mono records had used lateral movement to encode the waveform, which worked much better than vertical movement. The way stereo recording worked was that two voice coils were set at a 45 degree angle to each other, with one having its phase reversed so that they reinforced each other. Left and right signals were cut in the walls of the groove and stereo signals encoded. The advantage of the system at the time was that mono records could be played back happily on stereo record players. However, the reverse was a problem as mono record players would damage stereo records. To avoid damaging the vinyl, record companies used to produce both a stereo and mono version (right up to the 1970s).
- 1980s – Stereo television and VCR systems developed; with digital high definition now standard, stereo sound and surround sound were more widespread.

To get the best stereo experience, the sitting position of the listener in relation to the speakers is important. This position is known as 'the sweet spot'; it is where the listener is capable of hearing the full range of sound, as the mixing engineer originally intended it. The diagram below illustrates this point.

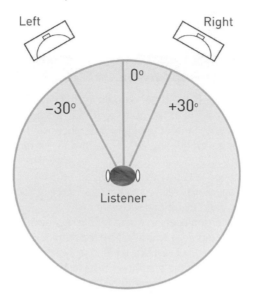

SURROUND SOUND

The development of this technology took place largely in the American film industry – although research also took place in the UK and France (notably in the Paris club, the Moulin Rouge in 1987). However, parallel developments took place in the home theatre industry after the development of DVD and blu-ray discs. Some important films to use surround sound formats are:

- Walt Disney's film *Fantasia* (1940); it is the first film to use surround sound
- The Who's rock opera *Tommy* (1975); it featured quadraphonic four-channel sound
- George Lucas' film *Star Wars* (1977); it uses Dolby Stereo, which despite its name employs four channels of audio. (It was particularly effective in the battle scenes when fighter planes would appear to fly across the theatre.)
- Tim Burton's *Batman Returns* (1992); Dolby debuts surround sound using their Dolby Digital system with the film
- Steven Spielberg's *Jurassic Park* (1993): DTS features 5.1 surround sound with the film
- Disney-Pixar's *Toy Story 3* (2010); it is released with 7.1 surround sound.

The diagram opposite illustrates 5:1 surround sound.

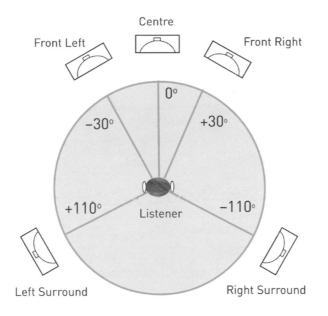

Centre

Front Left   Front Right

0°

−30°   +30°

+110°   −110°

Listener

Left Surround   Right Surround

Sound synthesis

UNDERSTANDING HARMONICS

A synthesiser is an instrument that can create sounds electronically. Technically, Hammond organs are synthesisers that use a method called additive synthesis to create new sounds. The Hammond sound is created by using drawbars to combine basic sine waves from the harmonic series (sounds that are inherent in any natural vibrating object). The stave below shows the natural overtones that are produced when C (below middle C) is played. These harmonic notes are not heard as pitches but rather as tone qualities or timbres of the fundamental note (in this case C). The C is heard as the pitch, because it is the note struck; the other notes resonate and are known as harmonics. As harmonics get higher they also get quieter; theoretically, they continue ascending infinitely.

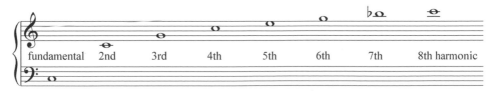

fundamental   2nd   3rd   4th   5th   6th   7th   8th harmonic

For a synthesiser the process begins when an oscillator creates a waveform. In subtractive synthesis the waveforms are harmonically rich – such as triangle or square waves (see table on pages 64–5) – so that filters can be applied to them. The following illustration shows the Steinberg Monologue analogue synthesiser virtual instrument, which shows the various controls commonly used in analogue sound shaping.

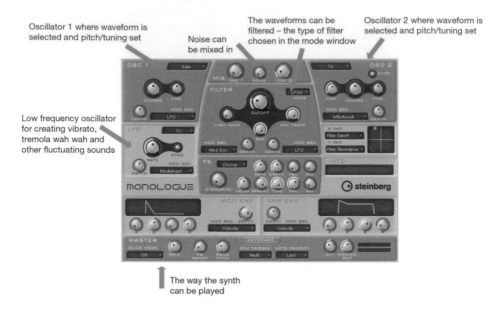

Oscillator 1 where waveform is selected and pitch/tuning set

Noise can be mixed in

The waveforms can be filtered – the type of filter chosen in the mode window

Oscillator 2 where waveform is selected and pitch/tuning set

Low frequency oscillator for creating vibrato, tremola wah wah and other fluctuating sounds

The way the synth can be played

WAVEFORMS

A list of waveforms is set out below:

Waveform	Graphic	Description
Sine		Simple, regular wave with pure sound; it is not used in subtractive synthesis, because if it was filtered there would be nothing left
Sawtooth		Edgy sound, ideal for string sounds
Triangle		Quiet harmonics

SECTION 1: EQUIPMENT IN CONTEXT

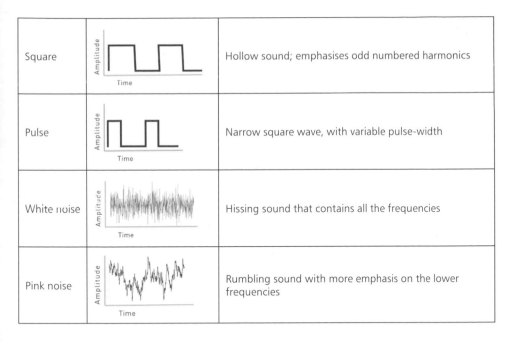

Square		Hollow sound; emphasises odd numbered harmonics
Pulse		Narrow square wave, with variable pulse-width
White noise		Hissing sound that contains all the frequencies
Pink noise		Rumbling sound with more emphasis on the lower frequencies

The waveforms are produced by a voltage controlled oscillator (VCO). Since the keyboards of most portable analogue synths are limited in length, there will be a switch for choosing which octave to use. Waveforms can be manipulated in a variety of ways:

1. **Filters** (VCF / voltage controlled filter) — there are three main types: low-pass, hi-pass and band-pass; as their names suggest, they filter out set areas of the waveform. For example, a low-pass allows the low sounds through but gradually removes the high sounds as the filter is applied. They use a cut-off frequency above or below where they take effect. They also have a resonance control, which increases the gain immediately around the cut-off frequency; this can produce howling sounds when set against a high frequency. The diagram below represents a resonant low-pass filter frequency response graph.

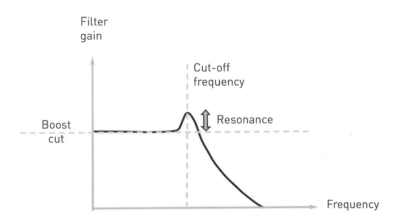

2. **Envelope shapers** – these are normally applied to amplitude (volume VCA) but can also include effect filters (VCF) or pitch (VCO). The standard envelope uses attack, decay, sustain and release (ADSR). In the 1970s, when synthesisers attempted to emulate real instruments, a brass sound would be synthesised with an attack portion for the almost immediate commencement of the sound. The decay imitates the initial lipping, the sustain imitates how long the note is held and a short release simulates how long the air vibrations take to die away. The following diagrams are a graphic representation of the sound levels produced over time for three acoustic instruments.

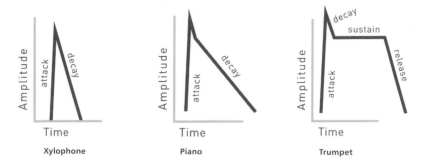

| Xylophone | Piano | Trumpet |

3. **Modulation** – these are regular changes in pitch, amplitude or timbre that are affected by a low frequency oscillator (LFO). A vibrato effect is achieved when a moderately fast time and a short pitch range is applied to the VCO. On the VCA, tremolo effects are produced, and wah-wah sounds can be imitated on the VCF.
4. **De-tuning** – common usage is to take more than one waveform and combine it with one set at a slightly different pitch, which creates an enriched result.
5. **Portamento** – this is when the pitch slides from one note to another rather than moving in steps; different types are available depending on how the keys are pressed.
6. **Monophonic effects** – for synths that can only produce one note at a time, playing techniques can be developed that cut off the preceding note. This is useful when trying to copy the sound of a monophonic instrument such as a trumpet, or it could be used to create interest in a mono lead solo.
7. **Polyphonic synths** – these produce several notes at once, so chords or pads (mellow sustained chord sounds) can be created.
8. **Arpeggiators** – some synths utilise built-in basic sequencers to create patterns of notes.
9. **White or pink noise** – these can be mixed in to the more musical waveforms to create more gritty sounds, particularly for instruments such as the drum or a saxophone.

PRECURSORS TO THE SYNTHESISER

1906: The Telharmonium was completed. This was a massive 200 ton instrument driven by 12 steam-powered electromagnetic generators; the music was piped into the public telephone network.

1920: The theremin – named after its Russian inventor – had no keyboard and the player would wave their hands between two antennae to create disturbances in an electrostatic field. It created a ghostly sound and was used by film composers to create atmosphere – for example, Miklos Rozsa's score for Hitchcock's 1945 film *Spellbound*.

1928: The ondes Martenot was invented. Frenchman Maurice Martenot demonstrated his invention to the Parisian public where it was a great success. It had a keyboard with a pull-out drawer that contained an articulation controller (the ancestors of the modern pitch and modulation wheels) and a ribbon controller, located directly under the keyboard. A number of French classical composers have used it in their scores, such as Messiaen, Honegger and Milhaud. It frequently turns up in popular music (for example, bands such as Radiohead), and film scores (such as *Lawrence of Arabia* in 1962 and *Ghostbusters* in 1984).

1931: The Rhythmicon is an early example of a drum machine. It consisted of a 17-note keyboard, which when pressed generated pulses of notes at a predetermined pitch; the 17th note allowed the insertion of rests to produce a syncopated effect. The other keys played a number of pulses worked out as an arithmetic progression: the first key would generate one pulse; the second key, two pulses over the same duration; the third, three pulses and so on. Any of the keys could be pressed at the same time so that combinations as complex as 15 notes against 16 could be performed. Complex patterns could be created, but it lacked the sharp attack of modern drum machines.

> After the invention of the transistor in 1947/8 electronic instruments became much more portable.

1964: The first of the generation of voltage controlled synthesisers was born when Robert Moog combined a voltage-controlled oscillator and an amplifier module with a keyboard. The modular system was still a cumbersome instrument, although more manageable than the huge synthesisers of the past which were used in the experimental electronic music studios in Paris and Cologne. Nevertheless, Wendy Carlos's album *Switch on Bach* (1968) was a huge commercial success and persuaded many studios to take an interest in Moog's instruments. It was also one of the first multitracked albums and set a record for sales of a classical album by retailing more than 500,000 units. The modular system required the player to connect the various components together using patch leads. For example, if vibrato was required, a modulation generator would be connected to the VCO (voltage controlled oscillator) using a cable and regular variations in pitch would then be produced. Below is a picture of the Moog Modular Synthesiser M55.

1970: Moog realised that performing musicians would prefer an instrument that didn't require its player to possess an engineering degree in order to get some sound out of it. He put together a synth that had its connections hard-wired in the factory; it was much cheaper and more portable. It was known as the Minimoog and became the best selling analogue synth of all time. It had excellent quality filters, and three oscillators that could be individually tuned and set to a number of waveforms. The synth was only monophonic but by using detuning and combining waveforms the oscillators could create a very rich sound. The Minimoog is now a collector's item.

Polyphony: The next major development in synthesiser history was the ability to play more than one note at a time – polyphony. Some synthesisers used a separate monophonic synth for each note of the keyboard, such as the Polymoog. Others used the idea that a synthesiser was attached to a note only when a key was pressed – this system became the norm.

1978: Musicians also wanted the ability to store the sounds they created and recall them quickly on stage. One of the earliest synths that featured both patch storage and polyphonic performance (in this case five voice) was Sequential Circuits Prophet-5.

1979: Expensive sampling keyboards were introduced: the Synclavier and the Fairlight CMI (pictured below) used digital technology to edit their sounds.

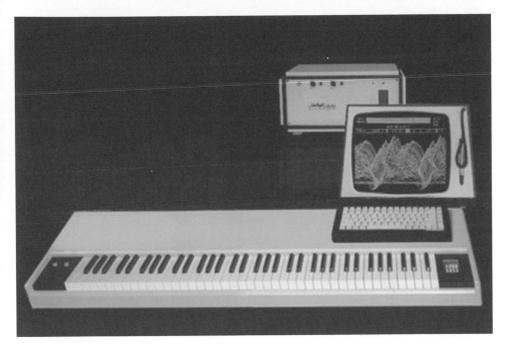

1980s: With the advent of true digital synthesisers and the rapid increase in computing power, polyphonic synths could cope with an increasing amount of polyphony; 16-note polyphony was the standard by the end of the decade.

1983: The first affordable digital synthesiser to appear on the market was the Yamaha DX7, which used a type of sound production called FM synthesis. Based on the principle of FM radio, pure sine waves are generated called operators which combine together in different orders. The DX7 had six operators, touch sensitivity and a removable e-prom where sounds could be stored.

Digital synthesisers produced a high level of realism when attempting to imitate acoustic instruments. FM synthesisers created great sounding bells and tuned percussion, as well as very passable wind instruments. Untuned percussion sounded a little artificial. Editing the sounds was difficult compared with the hands-on knobs and dials of traditional synths, as each parameter of the sound was numeric and had to be entered and saved. Fortunately preset locations and removable storage media was provided.

Although the recreation of acoustic instruments was much more realistic, the warm rich sounds and the quick onstage editing of analogue synths was not available on the DX7. Nevertheless the instrument was hugely popular and became the best selling synth of all time. New sounds could be created before doing a gig: MIDI implementation with software editing, plus cartridge storage of sounds for quick recall on stage, helped the musician cope with the mathematical complexities of FM. The metallic clean sounds it produced suited the music of the time. Below is a picture of the Yamaha DX7.

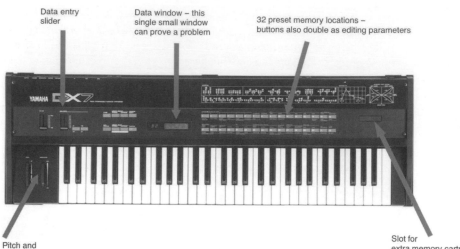

Data entry slider

Data window – this single small window can prove a problem

32 preset memory locations – buttons also double as editing parameters

Pitch and modulation wheels

Slot for extra memory cartridge

As MIDI implementation became common, synthesisers became capable of producing not just many notes at the same time but also many different sounds. This was ideal for use with sequencers, or for layering to produce rich soundscapes. Instruments with this capability were known as multitimbral.

Polyphonic analogue synths continued to be produced, with the following improvements: MIDI implementation; greater amounts of patch storage; the replacement of the VCO with a DCO (digitally controlled oscillator), which made pitch generation more stable. Examples of these models included the Roland Juno 106 and the Oberheim Matrix 6.

1987: The next development was in the area of S&S (sampling and synthesis). S&S methods were combined to create powerful new sounds. The idea was to sample just the attack portion of a waveform and then extend its length using analogue techniques, based on the idea that the human ear forms a judgement very quickly about the quality of an incoming sound. Roland's D50 used this in their LA Linear Arithmetic system in 1987. This combined 8-bit PCM samples and subtractive synthesis, and the instrument even had onboard chorus and digital reverb. In the following year (1988), the Kawai K1 and the Korg M1 were released, which both used similar sound production techniques.

Further developments took place with the use of sampled waves. This included the highly successful wavetable synthesis, which used large collections of digitally produced waveforms (say 64) to interact with each other.

1994: Yamaha's VL1 utilised complex computer algorithms known as physical modelling techniques to emulate the characteristics of acoustic sounds. Together with Korg, the company has pushed forward the boundaries of sound synthesis. However, nowadays hardware development is less important as attention has moved to software synths – which are downloadable, relatively cheap and highly manageable.

2003: Some synths had always had built-in sequencer capability (e.g. Jupiter 4 used by Duran Duran in their 1982 title track 'Rio') and also featured onboard signal processing and CD writers. These keyboards became known as synth workstations. They could be used to create music in home studios. The Yamaha Motif released in 2003 is a high end-version of a workstation.

Samplers and sampling

A sampler is a device that records audio either as single notes (one-shots), musical excerpts or acoustic noises. The device can process audio and store it ready for playback. A brief overview of the development of the sampler is set out in the table below.

1963	The Mellotron was released – a precursor to the sampler. It used tape recordings to playback sounds; it was a favourite instrument of many bands including the Beatles
1969	EMS Musys produced – the first digital sampler
1979	Fairlight CMI produced – the first polyphonic digital sampler
1987	E-mu SP-1200 percussion sampler – much favoured by hip-hop artists
1987	Roland D50 – the first affordable synthesiser to use sample playback in combination with sound synthesis
1988	Akai S100 – the first professional-quality 16-bit stereo sampler
1998	Gigasampler software released – this initiated the gradual decline of hardware samplers
2000s	Most sampling is now integrated into sequencing software such as Logic and Cubase
2010	Propellerhead's Reason 5 software environment included a special software sampler named NN-19 (pictured below)

KEY FACTS

Key facts about samplers:

- Samplers can record audio digitally and then store it in RAM (random access memory) for recall and editing
- They normally have settable sample rates and bit-depth (see page 8)
- Historically, samplers were part of a keyboard system or a rack-mounted unit that was triggered externally
- Software samplers often focus on the playback of preset samples rather than spending their energy on sample editing and recording, unless they are built into a DAW (digital audio workstation) where recording facilities already exist.

EDITING SAMPLES

The table below provides details on how recorded samples can be edited and then saved for later recall.

Sample edit	Using cut and paste.
Truncating	Editing the start and end points for a clean sample.
Looping	The sample repeats to either increase its sustaining length or create a real-time rhythmic pattern. Triggering a rhythmic pattern from a different note changes its speed of playback: for example, an octave higher doubles its speed. The loop point is settable and the sampler can calculate the best place to return to, in order to get the best match and avoid a click for a sustained sound. The sampler will search through the sample for a zero level that can serve as a loop point.
Zone allocation	Multiple samples can be stored and triggered from different areas of the same keyboard or on the same MIDI channel. This is useful as the sample playback changes its character when played very much higher or lower.
Velocity layering	Different samples are assigned to respond to varying velocity levels: for example, a brighter sounding sample of the same instrument could be triggered when a key is depressed with high velocity.
Processing	Filters and modulation can be applied using synthesis techniques.
Sample reverse	The recordings can be played backwards.
Synthesis techniques	Parameters such as attack and release time can be changed: for example, with a long release time, a rhythmic sample can be left to complete its pattern after only a short stab on the keyboard.
Sample rate change	The original sample rate can be changed to match other systems. CD quality sample rates are set by the Red Book Standard at 44.1kHz and 16 bit. Lower sample rates produce a lower quality of sound but also have a gritty quality that is sometimes sought after.
Time stretching	The length of the sample is changed without altering the pitch.

Large amounts of memory are available on modern samplers and computer-based software samplers. Phrase samplers can record whole sections of music, which allows performers to build up interesting textures.

> The first part of a sample can be repeated by multiple triggering, as in 'Imma Be' by The Black Eyed Peas.

Other keyboards

A distinction must be made between electric and electronic. The first refers to instruments that produce their sound using acoustic mechanical methods but employ electricity to help with this. The second term describes instruments that actually generate their sound by using electronic processes, employing analogue oscillators or digital technologies.

ELECTRIC PIANOS

Electric pianos have real hammers that, instead of hitting strings like an acoustic piano, hit thin metal reeds or thin wires called tines. Their vibrations are then sensed by pickups like an electric guitar and sent to an amplifier for further processing. The reeds can be tuned by either filing them down to make them sharper or dripping solder on to make them flatter. The sound can be either rich and mellow if played gently, or more cutting and metallic when played with force; the position of the pickup can be altered, which will also change the tone. Because of the lack of iron frame for the strings, electric pianos are much more portable than an acoustic piano.

The most famous makes of electric piano are the Wurlitzer and the Fender Rhodes. Examples of the Wurlitzer in use include Ray Charles 'What'd I Say' (1959), Supertramp's 'Dreamer' from the album *Crime of the Century* (1974), and Queen's 'You're My best Friend' from *Night At The Opera* (1975). The Fender Rhodes (pictured below) was a particular favourite of jazz musicians and known for its mellow sound.

Hohner produced an electric clavichord named the clavinet; Yamaha, Baldwin and Kawai made electric pianos that actually amplified wire strings and sounded more like an acoustic piano.

ELECTRONIC PIANOS

Early electronic pianos were not touch sensitive; instead they produced their sound through oscillators like a synthesiser. The 300 Series Electra-piano, made by Rocky Mount Instruments, was used in the 1970s by prog rock bands such as Genesis. Digital pianos were born in 1984 with the Kurzweil 250 – a portable keyboard with a huge range of sounds and facilities. Digital pianos can be considered as ROM (read only memory) sample players. They use multi-sampled recordings of real pianos (stored in ROM) which are triggered by velocity sensitive keys. They normally have several sets of samples available, a range of pianos together with strings and organ sounds. MIDI in and outs are frequently provided and therefore the keyboards can be used to access sound modules or connect to computers. Some models include lead-weighted keys, with gravity returns, instead of springs; this offers the musician a more realistic touch. Additional features include headphone outputs and transposition.

THE HAMMOND ORGAN

This innovative instrument has been around since the 1930s, but its heyday was during the 1950s and 1960s. It started life as a church organ. However, because of the innovative way it produced its sound it found its way into other fields of music. The B-3 model was used first as a jazz instrument with players like Jimmy Smith, creating exciting instrumental albums of blues and bebop before it moved into pop music. Booker T and the MGs had a memorable hit with 'Green Onions' (1962), which featured an organ playing lead for a simple 12-bar blues. The Hammond organ was used by the band Procul Harum to play a famous Bach-like lead verse for their 1967 hit 'A Whiter Shade of Pale'. It was also a favourite instrument for the American west coast surf style and the heavy rock bands of the 1970s.

The Hammond employs a series of drawbars mounted on the right side of the console on smaller models, coloured black, brown and white. The black ones are tuned to the notes you would expect but in different octaves. Therefore if you played C, a C note would be produced; its octave and volume level would depend on which of the black drawbars was extended and how far it was pulled out. The other drawbars were tuned to other notes of the harmonic series and were used to colour the sound, so that if large numbers of these were extended the tone would become more nasal.

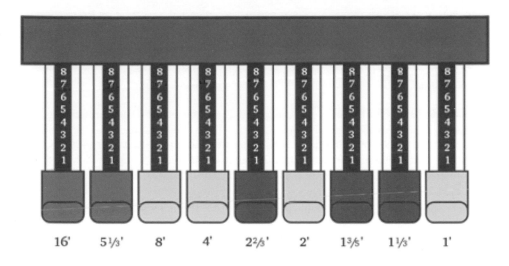

| 16' | 5⅓' | 8' | 4' | 2⅔' | 2' | 1³⁄₅' | 1⅓' | 1' |

Sound production is via mechanical tonewheels that rotate in front of electromagnetic pickups, as shown in the illustration below.

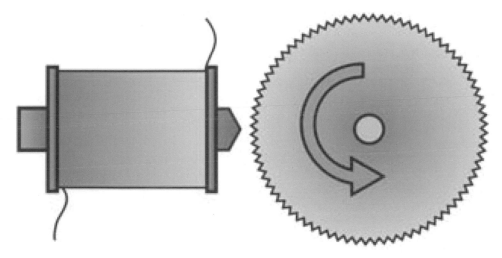

This way of producing new sounds – by adding sine waves of various pitches – is known technically as additive synthesis. The organ also had the facility of providing an emphasised envelope to a note so that it quickly decayed. This is known as harmonic percussion. It allowed players to emulate a piano or guitar envelope and other instruments that also have a quick decay at the start of their notes. Unlike these acoustic instruments however, the effect would only be repeated when all the notes of a chord (or a set of legato notes) had been released. In the hands of experienced Hammond players, it was possible to achieve some very expressive effects.

The Hammond organ featured two manuals (keyboards) plus an octave of foot pedal notes. The normal way of playing would be to set the sound of the top manual and use it with the right hand as the lead part, while setting the sound quieter for the left hand to use as an accompaniment on the lower manual. Expression could also be achieved with a right foot 'swell' control; the left foot was occupied with the bass pedals.

Although the organ had a built-in amplifier and speaker, it was often sent through a Leslie Cabinet. This was an external amplifier and speaker that contained a rotating horn, with the player having the choice of a fast (tremolo) or slow (chorale). This projected the sound out using the physics of the Doppler effect, creating a characteristic slight shift in pitch and changes in volume and tone according to the direction that the horn was facing.

There are a number of plug-ins on the market that emulate vintage keyboards and synths. The Hammond organ (pictured below), various electric pianos and vintage synths are well represented.

Electric guitars

Guitar-like instruments have been around since antiquity but the modern, six string version can be traced back to the 19th century. The electric guitar was born in the 1930s. Since then, famous electric guitar brands have included Fender, Rickenbacker, Gibson and Gretsch.

There is a wide variety of guitar body-shapes available, semi acoustic designs (for example, Epiphone guitars) and solid wood (for example, Fender Stratocaster). Some employ tremolo arms that are fixed to the bridge; these can alter the tension of the strings to create vibrato effects. Different gauges (weights) of strings are available, with rock players preferring light gauge (easier to bend) and jazz players using heavy gauge (richer sound). Also available on the market is a 12-string guitar and a double-necked guitar; these extend the playing possibilities even further.

Electric guitars use a variety of pickups. These are coils of fine wire around a magnet that pick up the vibrations of the metal strings and convert the disturbances of the magnetic field into electrical energy. The movement of a diaphragm in a dynamic microphone works in the same way. Most guitars have three pickups that are placed in different positions under the strings; each pickup has the ability to be controlled individually to produce varying tones.

Single coil pickups (found on guitars such as the Fender Telecaster) produce a twangy, slightly thin sound. In contrast, Humbucker pickups have two coils; because they cover a wider section of the string their tone is thicker and more powerful. Two coil pickups can be used to reduce the hum that traditional single coil types can create, and they also avoid picking up interference from other magnetic sources. This is because the two coils are wound in opposite directions and use phase cancellation to reduce the noise.

Another type of pickup uses piezoelectric technology and is sometimes built into the bridge. As this is not magnetic it creates quite a different sound and requires battery power to function.

Sometimes electric guitars have a preamplifier between the pickup and the cable. This is also battery powered and the high output produced can also be shaped by filters and EQ; it is known as an active pickup. Many of the more expensive bass guitars feature active pickups because of the clean, clear sound they produce.

An able guitar player can produce a large number of effects to enhance the various playing styles. Harmonics and feedback techniques are particularly successful given the high volumes used on stage, and there are a huge range of foot pedals available, some that can be linked together into convenient cases which can process the sound in live performance.

EFFECTS PEDALS

The list below covers the variety of effects pedals available on the market:

- Distortion pedals – such as a fuzz box
- Sustain pedals – these use compression to boost dying signals gradually and create long held sounds
- Delay processors – hold back the sound and echo it back at set intervals, sometimes timed to fit with the music
- Chorus and doubling – create the illusion of there being more than one player.

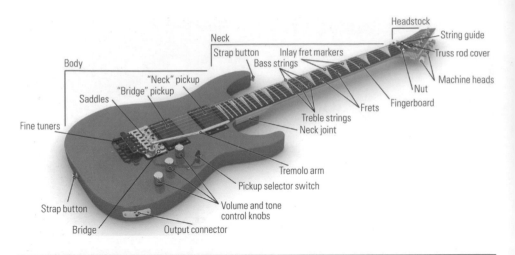

Sequencers, MIDI and audio

EARLY SEQUENCERS

Modern sequencers handle both MIDI and audio signals with ease – but it hasn't always been that way. Sequencers record data in a linear fashion for editing and playback. The earliest machines of this type could be said to be automated mechanical devices such as music boxes and barrel organs.

In 1959, Wurlitzer produced the first commercial drum machine known as the Sideman. A drum machine takes drums sounds and arranges them in order so it is in fact a type of sequencer.

> Step sequencing is an arranging technique where the notes and their durations are entered into a sequencer's memory one at a time, as opposed to real-time sequencing where the notes are played in.

In 1968 Robert Moog enhanced his successful 1964 modular synthesiser with several new modules, including the 960 Step Sequencer (pictured below). This used voltages to control the opening and closing of gates sent from a keyboard or by using internal clock oscillators. The 960 Step Sequencer was able to set duration, pitch and skip notes, and used three VCOs so it could produce three note chords. However, it required a lot of programming to be used to its full potential.

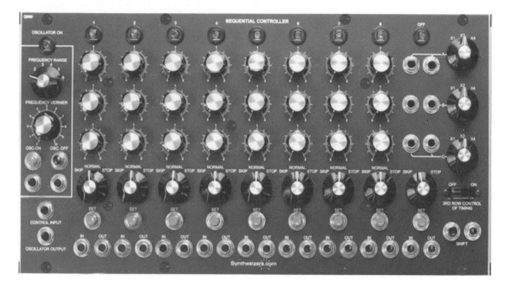

All early sequencers of this type used step-time programming – i.e. note, pitch and duration data was entered before the music could be played back. However, some imaginative bands could change the switches during performance, adding or dropping notes from a previously prepared looped sequence – for example, Tangerine Dream's album *Phaedra* (1974). Step sequencers were built into a number of popular analogue synths during the 1970s; the regular musical loops became a feature of the synthpop style. They are still very popular in electronic dance styles, especially the trance music of the 1990s with its rapid arpeggios and minor scale patterns.

A number of companies produced digitally controlled analogue sequencers, which used voltage control in combination with computer memory. One such model was the Roland MC-8 MicroComposer (released in 1977), which was a convenient stand-alone unit. During the late 1970s and early '80s, sampling workstations such as the Synclavier and Fairlight featured step sequencers. However, the advent of MIDI in 1983 moved sequencers in a new direction.

MIDI

The common digital language of MIDI enabled not just synthesisers and sound modules to connect up, but also a link to a computer could be established (although MIDI was too basic a digital language to actually represent audio signals). The Atari ST had built-in MIDI connections and so was one of the first computers to have music software specially written for its operating system. In 1984 Charlie Steinberg created his Pro-16 MIDI sequencer. The software was initially for the Commodore 64 computer, but it soon migrated to the Atari in the form of the Pro-24. This version introduced the concept of quantisation, where timing errors could be corrected. Quantisation was necessary because these software systems allowed the user to record their music in real time. In version 2 of Pro-24, score editing became possible. In 1985, Mark Of The Unicorn released their Digital Performer software for the Apple Mac computer but the sequences had to be saved and imported into another programme for score editing.

C-lab Notator software arrived from Germany near the end of 1988 and was a big step forward. The sequenced music and the notation were totally integrated, enabling notes on a score to be dragged up and down to different staff lines, while the user could hear the results instantaneously. The image below is a screenshot from Atari Notator.

The different tracks

MIDI functions of the selected track (in this case the Sound fx track)

The sections of the music as it progresses

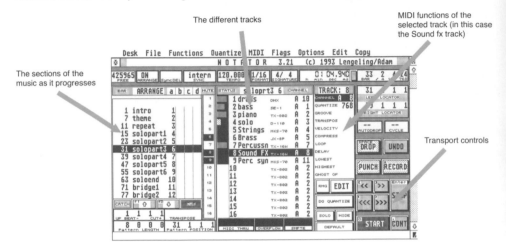

Transport controls

Tracker software developed alongside MIDI sequencing. This enabled short samples to be arranged in a linear way against a grid. It was popular on the Commodore Amiga computer because of its more advanced sound chip. (Originally, only 8-bit samples could be sequenced on four channels.) The software soon moved to the PC, making use of PCI sound cards such as the Sound Blaster series. At the time, computer games often employed this method of music composition.

Below is a summary of how MIDI capability advanced towards the end of the 20th century:

1983	The official MIDI 1.0 detailed specification was published
1986	The MIDI Sample Dump Standard was added to the MIDI specification
1987	MIDI Time Code was added (MTC)
1991	General Midi Standard was added, so that each sound/instrument was assigned to a specific number (0–127). It was particularly useful for sharing files between users, so that the MIDI file could be played back using different equipment and preserve the original sound allocations (instruments). MIDI files are also very small. These two factors meant that MIDI files played a large contribution in the development of sharing music on the internet.
1999	General MIDI 2 extensions were added to the MIDI spec. This increased the number of available sounds and control options. For example, General MIDI 2 enabled control for reverb, chorus and tuning.

See pages 38–40 for more detail of MIDI specifications.

AUDIO SOFTWARE DEVELOPMENT

In 1991 Steinberg released Cubase Audio and the following year E-magic produced Logic Audio. Both of these programs depended on external devices for their audio. In 1996, Cubase VST (virtual studio technology) was released, which had audio totally integrated, complete with on-screen mixing with effects. It also featured the ability to use audio plug-ins, including many developed by third parties – this became a standard file format still used today for both digital signal processing and virtual instruments.

Music on the internet

Computing power has increased substantially over the last decade. The availability of global broadband has made music downloading and storage of audio files on remote servers not just a possibility but the preferred way of working. This has had consequences for the high street record store and even domestic playback equipment. Smart phones with internet access can carry music and huge numbers of remotely stored files wherever the listener goes; even the famous Apple iPod is no longer the preferred music player.

File sharing on peer-to-peer networks is undermining the recording industry; artists now frequently post their demo tracks online to publicise their work. There have been a number of legal battles fought over the copyright infringement issue of file sharing. Original audio-file sharing companies such as Napster and Audiogalaxy have been closed down, or reborn as online retailers with a price tag attached to each track. Other companies have been highly successful as pay sites. For example, iTunes (launched in 2001) was originally an Apple-only application, but it is now available for Windows. To compete with the monopoly that iTunes held for purchasing audio downloads, Spotify (launched in 2008) is now a strong contender in the market.

UNDERSTANDING CODECS

Part of the success of internet music has been due to the various compression codecs used. (Note: compression in this context is not related to dynamic compression in signal processing.) File formats such as .wav or .aiff are too large for storage in vast quantities and take too long to download. With research into auditory masking and perceptual coding in the 1970s, it was realised that the human ear rejects a good deal of information and it will not be able to hear all of the information present in a recording. Therefore, it became possible to reduce the overall size of the file by filtering out sounds that were not being heard by the listener. Various codecs were invented, the most common in use today being listed below:

- MP3 – released in 1993 and the most popular of all compression codecs. If set at 128kbits, it will reduce a CD standard file to 1/11th of its original size. It is a lossy compression format but audio can be compressed at 10:1 without noticeable loss in quality. When encoding audio to MP3, a number of sample frequencies and bit-rates are available to choose from depending on the quality required (e.g.44.100kHz sample frequency and 256kbps or 320kbps bit rate). The format can carry additional information such as track listings and artists.

- WMA (Windows media audio) – released in 1999, it was developed by Microsoft as part of their Windows operating system. In 2003, Microsoft released a professional lossless codec for professional use.
- AAC (advanced audio coding) – recognized as slightly higher quality sound than MP3, when using the same bit rate. This is achieved largely through more highly efficient processes. AAC is the standard for Youtube, iPhone, iPod, iTunes (mp4a) and Playstation 3.
- Real Audio – released in 1995 and used for streaming audio, i.e. the music can be played while it downloads. Used in the past by the BBC websites until 2009 and the BBC world service until 2011.
- Ogg Vorbis – released in 2002, this codec produces a particularly high quality sound and is part of a free open source development. It is popular with video game developers and used for streaming by Spotify. The small sized files relative to the audio quality make them suitable for all web applications.

Section 2: the exam

Unit 4

The examination for *Unit 4: Analysing and Producing* is divided into two sections: Section A and Section B. It covers a total of five questions, which are to be completed within two hours. Two CDs are provided with the exam paper: one contains the audio and (possibly MIDI) data that you are expected to import and manipulate; the second CD is blank for you to burn the wav files that you have created during the exam. If you are given just one CD with the exam paper, it will be the data disc and you do not need to worry about burning the final CD.

> The burning of the wav files to CD does not need to take place during the two hours of exam time and can be completed by a technician. However, it is your responsibility to ensure that the wav files have been exported correctly and have been saved to the correct place. Your teacher/technician is not permitted to export any wav files from your DAW or adjust them in any way.

Section A	Contains four questions and will guide you through what you need to do with the audio/MIDI data on the exam CD.
Section B	Contains only one question (question 5). This question is always split into six parts; it requires you to create a stereo mix, following specific instructions. The final mix will be approximately one minute in length.

All five questions in the exam will be split into multiple parts to test the following four main areas:

- Identifying key musical features
- Identifying the use of music technology
- Historical knowledge of music technology
- Practical application of music technology.

1: Identifying key musical features

These questions will test your ability to identify general musical characteristics and devices present in the audio. Typical questions will include a general understanding of the aspects of music theory that are pertinent to a music technology student. These include:

- Understanding pitch and rhythm in drum and staff notation (bass and treble clefs)
- Identifying keys and chords
- Knowledge of standard Italian terms for dynamics, tempo, articulation and playing techniques.

TYPICAL QUESTIONS

As part of this element, you will be required to compare an audio track with staff notation presented in the exam paper. You will be asked to identify and correct pitch and rhythm errors. You may also be asked to name specific performance techniques exemplified in the audio on the data disc.

Brushing up on music theory
To help you prepare for this question, access some of the online drills or games available on the internet. The website www.emusictheory.com offers free music theory drills, which provide a choice of exercises at different levels of difficulty. There are many other websites that provide similar services: a search for 'music reading games' will produce several useable links.

It is also common to find a question that asks you to identify the notes in a chord or the key of the music. Drills can help practise these listening skills as well. You are likely to be asked whether a chord or the music's key is either major or minor, or based on a mode such as dorian or aeolian; whether a chord has an extension (e.g. a 7th); and whether its root note is in the bass.

2: Identifying the use of music technology

In Unit 2 (AS level), this area was mostly restricted to identifying the way technology was used in the tracks on the exam CD. In Unit 4 you are still expected to be able to identify the use of technology as heard on the audio and MIDI extracts on the data CD. However, at A2 you are also expected to be able to think about the use of technology in a more abstract way, being able to discuss various parameters without necessarily having heard them first. For example, you may be asked a question about compression that requires you to discuss various important controls on a compressor, or you may be asked about specific MIDI or audio editing features that you have learned about while you were completing Units 1 and 3 (the coursework). Overall, this area can be thought of as combining your theoretical and practical knowledge of music technology.

Help can be found for the full range of topics in section 1 of this book.

TYPICAL QUESTIONS

Below is a list of questions you could expect to encounter:

- How would you mic up an electric guitar?
- How would you create the impression of double tracking on the guitar part?
- Describe how MIDI controllers have been used in the synth pad part in bars 9–15.

- What modulation effect has been applied to the vocal part at the end of the track?
- Give two advantages and two disadvantages of DI recording.
- Draw a line on the graph to illustrate the effects of a compressor set with a threshold of -10 dB and a compression ratio of 3:1,
- Complete the table to link cable types with their connection functions.

3: Historical knowledge

To prepare further for the essay in question 4, pages 98–104 provide exemplar questions and answers.

Historical knowledge is examined in question 4, the essay question. Any of the areas covered in this revision guide on the development of technology-based music (Area of Study 3) could come up. It is possible to approach these questions either from a historical angle without knowing many technical facts, or from a technical angle without remembering many chronological developments. However, to score high marks you need both technical terms and understanding. Question 4 will probably have nothing whatsoever to do with the audio provided on the CD.

There will be a choice of two contrasting questions on the development of music technology. It is sensible to choose the question you know most about.

The subject matter for these may come from the following list:

Development of:

- Synthesisers
- Electric guitars and amplification
- Samplers and drum machines
- Use of effects units and processors across time
- Development of recording media including multitrack recording.

Digital recording, including awareness of:

- Computer-based recording (including knowledge of typical software packages)
- Hard disc/standalone recorders
- Computer-hosted virtual instruments/effects
- The impact of MIDI on recording and performing
- Use of the internet as both a resource and for communication between artists
- The context of all the above and the impact of technology on producers, engineers and artists.

Questions 2 and 3 require you to import further tracks into your sequencer. Care must be taken to import the tracks exactly where they are supposed to go. Often a sequencer will import audio at the point where the playback cursor is positioned at the time. Therefore, it is a good idea to have the cursor correctly positioned first before you import. You can move the audio file to the correct position after it is imported. However, this method risks that the file might not snap to the right place; if snap is turned off, for example, subtle timing differences may result.

> Snap is a function that forces tracks to begin at the global quantise setting – for example, at a $\frac{1}{16}$th or $\frac{1}{8}$th note or at a half bar.

In Unit 2, the 'practical' application of music technology was still theoretical – you had to think about what you might have done in a given situation. (For example, how you would have recorded an upright piano?) In Unit 4, you actually have to do things with the given audio. Questions 1, 2 and 3 will ask you to import the different tracks from the data CD and to do something with them.

Below is a selection of editing tasks that you might be asked to perform:

- Finding suitable timbres for the MIDI part(s)
- An element of synthesis to be utilised in the MIDI part(s)
- Correcting problems with the loop points – for example, trimming the samples
- Assembling tracks from the audio loops
- Removing unwanted noise
- Correcting errors in the MIDI/audio performance
- Adjusting the MIDI performance in some way:
    - Applying quantisation
    - Changing the note lengths
    - Adding other notes – for example, additional octaves, filling out chords and so on
    - Altering the groove
- Applying specific processes to the audio:
    - EQ
    - Filtering
    - Compression/limiting
    - Gating
    - Pitch correction/transposition
    - Panning
    - Reverb
    - Delay
    - Other specific effects – for example, chorus, flanger, enhancer, distortion, ADT and so on
    - Re-amping a part that has been recorded using DI techniques.

The exam paper will be very precise in the instructions it gives you. Follow the instructions to the letter and don't try to apply additional creativity, as you will gain no extra marks and waste time. For example, if you were commissioned to compose a 25 second clip for a commercial, the producers would not be impressed if you were creative with the timings! Similarly, you are expected to do exactly what the exam paper asks you to do.

KNOWING YOUR SOFTWARE

EDITING MIDI

MIDI and audio editing can be time consuming and fiddly, so it would be wise to spend some revision time looking at the many shortcuts provided by the various sequencers around. It is likely you will have used them in your coursework.

For example, MIDI editing using Cubase is quick and easy. MIDI functions include provide detail editing of:

- Legato
- Down-beat accents
- The logical editor allows the user to focus on specific parameters and transform them to something else
- Selection tools can help pick out exactly which MIDI notes are to be affected
- Masking the information that is not needed in the list editor allows selection of, for example, the pitch bend elements for quick deletion or change.

The examination expects a great deal of practical work in a limited time so any technique that can help repetitive tasks is very useful.

AUDIO EDITING

You will be expected to edit the imported files. You will have to cut and splice the files, so it is a good idea to be familiar with your software's preferences settings. For example:

- In Logic Pro 9, choosing 'Preferences>General>Editing>Limit dragging to one direction> arrange' will stop you accidentally dragging your edited region in two dimensions.
- In Cubase 4, a similar restraint is applied when holding the command key on a Mac or the ctrl key on a Windows machine.

Splicing audio files

A zero crossing is where the audio waveform crosses from positive to negative.

When splicing two audio files together, offensive clicks or glitches can be detected if there is a displacement or mismatch between the waveforms of the two parts. If there is a zero crossing where the files join then there is no problem. If the two files overlap they need to be crossfaded, that is one part fades out while the other fades in. By selecting two consecutive overlapping audio events in Cubase and pressing X an automatic crossfade is created. The illustration below shows the effects of using two different editing points.

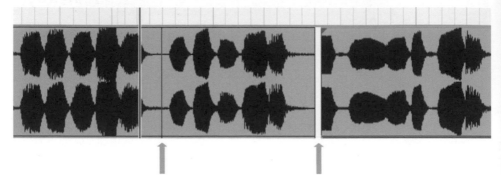

Edit point 1 : no problem   Edit point 2 : will cause click

Fade in and outs can be created in Logic by dragging the fade tool over the start or end point of a region, or in Cubase by dragging the blue handles. Very short X-fade times need to be used to prevent noticeable phasing.

Adding an audio effect

If you are asked to apply an audio effect to a clip you must decide whether to use a send bus, an insert point, or to actually process the audio. If you are actually processing your audio, use any preview function available in your software to make sure the end result is what you require, before you make any permanent changes.

> It is important that you are familiar with the audio editing functions in your particular software. When working in detail, it is a good idea to increase the image size of the wave file, both vertically and horizontally using the adjustment buttons at the edge of the arrange window.

Removing unwanted noise

A common task asked for in questions 2 or 3 is to select an audio track and remove unwanted noise. Tight edit points are important for this task. Also, be careful not to introduce extra clicks. There are a number of ways to remove unwanted noise, as follows:

1. Use an insert to apply a noise gate to the track. Care must be taken to set the threshold so that the unwanted sound is cut out while the music is unaffected. The attack and decay settings can also affect how well the gate works.

2. Select the portion of the audio file where the noise is occurring and reduce the gain to an inaudible level.
3. Use a graphic EQ or notch filter to target the offensive sound. This may need to be on/off automated to avoid it affecting the rest of the audio track.

Types of questions you can expect

The exam style will remain the same from year to year, including a mix of different question types. Each type of question requires a specific approach in order to increase your chances of gaining maximum marks.

MULTIPLE CHOICE

There will always be a correct answer and (probably) an obviously incorrect answer. If you are unsure of the correct response, eliminate the options one by one in a logical fashion. If you think you have spotted an overall pattern in the multiple-choice responses (for example, A A B B C C D D), it will be completely by chance. (The exam board never arranges the answers like this deliberately.) The options are always listed in alphabetical, numerical or some other obvious order.

Put a cross in one box only – never give multiple responses or you will get zero credit. If you make an error, make it really clear what your intended correct response is supposed to be.

SINGLE-WORD RESPONSES (AND FILL-IN-THE-BLANKS QUESTIONS)

The examiner is not trying to trick you – if it sounds like an obvious response, then it probably is! Do not try to justify a one-word response or explain your answer. Make a considered response to the question, using appropriate musical or technical vocabulary when appropriate and then move on to the next question.

SHORT RESPONSE

These may appear as questions with one or two lines in which to present your answer. The number of lines given is an indication of how full your response should be. Make a careful note of how many marks are awarded for the question – this will let you know how many points you need to make. (The question itself may also indicate the number of points you should make to gain full marks.) Do not waffle: keep everything factual and to the point. Concise answers that use technical vocabulary score more highly than lengthy, waffly answers. If there are any words in bold type in the question, you **must** refer to them in your response or it is unlikely that you will score any marks.

EXTENDED RESPONSE

There won't be any extended response questions in the exam except for the essay question (question 4). This question offers 16 marks; it requires at least 16 creditworthy points arranged in a logical fashion. It is important that you use technical terms and musical/music technology vocabulary where appropriate in this question. It is also important that you spell the key words correctly. Some marks are awarded for 'buzzwords', but only if these words are spelled correctly and used in the appropriate context. As with any extended response question, it is the content that is important, not the quantity. Examiners hate waffle because it is almost always used to try and mask a lack of real knowledge. There is much more depth on question 4 in the next section of this chapter.

TABLE COMPLETION

These are the same as short-response or single-word questions. However, they are presented in a table to make it slightly easier to see exactly what the examiners are looking for. Ensure that your responses are in the correct columns. Tables are often given with an example row shaded at the top of the table. Try to use the same sort of language in your responses, with the same amount of depth and technical vocabulary.

STAFF NOTATION AND SPOT THE ERRORS

'Spot the error' questions tend to replace the notation-based questions from Unit 2. However, if they are quite short (i.e. identifying errors in pitch *or* rhythm, but not both), there will probably be another question that requires you to fill in some notation. For example:

- Complete the rhythm (often part of the drum track)
- Complete the melody (filling in the missing notes)
- Write out the chords in staff notation.

Any notation questions other than the 'spot the error' questions will be limited in how many marks they are worth. 'Spot the error' questions require you to find where the staff notation does not match up with what you can hear in the audio and then for you to suggest what the correct staff notation should be. You can't predict what parts the errors will be in before the exam begins (they will change from year to year), but all will be clearly laid out in the exam paper.

ANNOTATE THE DIAGRAM

In the exam it is possible for a question to be presented as a diagram or graph, which you then need to label or annotate. Diagrams will always be something that you should be familiar with from your experience of completing the coursework.

Possible examples include:

- EQ graph – perhaps a microphone/speaker response curve or a graph similar to what you would see in your sequencer's EQ section
- Compressor response curve
- Filter graph
- Reverb response graph
- The front panel of an effects unit (hardware or software) – this would either be a classic piece of equipment with well recognised controls or a generic device that could be used in any DAW
- Common waveform (e.g. sine wave, sawtooth wave and so on).

It is also possible that a diagram or picture could be used as the stimulus for a question; you may need to refer to certain attributes from the diagram/picture and explain them rather than labelling the diagram/picture itself.

PRACTICAL QUESTIONS

As mentioned previously, there is a significant proportion of this exam that will require you to manipulate audio/MIDI data. Before the exam, you should ensure that you are familiar with all the editing tasks covered in this revision guide to give you the best chance of scoring top marks. It is essential that you have familiarised yourself with past exam papers or practice papers before your real exam.

Mixing for question 5

There are a number of established practices used by mixing engineers; the different sections of the exam question will guide you through the mixing process. It cannot be emphasised enough that you should read question 5 carefully and carry out its instructions to the letter. This question is not designed to test your skill as an innovative producer, but rather to find out if you understand mixing processes well enough to reach a specific outcome. Your work is assessed as a whole mix, so it is important that all of the processing undertaken is audible and works in the context of the mix.

POSSIBLE PRACTICAL TASKS

By looking at the past papers available, it is possible to deduce the likely breakdown of the different parts of question 5, although there is always the possibility of a change in the next paper, so this list shouldn't be considered exhaustive. To date, there have been six areas covered (in no particular order):

1. Dynamic processing – asking you to compress particular tracks or add a noise gate and giving you advice and instructions on how this should be done.

2. EQ – asking you to EQ or apply a filter to a particular track, part of a track, or a number of tracks to produce a different tone.
3. Stereo processing – may include stereo double tracking and/or panning.
4. Effects – adding reverb, perhaps by different amounts to a track or a number of tracks.
5. Balance – blending the tracks together but ensuring that all can be heard.
6. Presentation of the mix – producing a final stereo mix, perhaps expecting set fades and asking for a high level output without distortion.

The final question (question 5) is worth 18 marks, or 14% of the entire paper. Take special care to ensure that the wav file for this question is presented as you intend it to be heard.

Adding reverb	When adding reverb, be sure to avoid a setting that will swamp everything and produce a sound like Westminster Abbey (unless this is asked for). The reverb type will most likely be given in the question. Be aware of the reverb tail so that the residual sound is not chopped off when you edit the ending. It is best to use an aux and the same reverb for whole mix as it is easier to control. Remember that you have to do this quickly in the exam.
Adding compression	It is easy to over-compress tracks (especially vocals) and kill any musical expression particularly in slower tempo music. Compression is important to help strengthen a sound and reduce the peaks, but not to create a monotonous dynamic. Get as close as possible to what you require and try adjusting the threshold. Listen carefully both with the track soloed and with the rest of the tracks playing; listen out for pumping or sudden unwanted drops in sound.
Using EQ	When using EQ, it is easier to hear the results by turning up the gain and sweeping the frequency. Be sure to turn down the gain when you have found the frequency you were searching for.
Hearing all parts	It is important that all the parts can be heard clearly throughout. There is no point having an instrument or voice in a mixdown of a song that cannot be heard clearly. All it will do is make the final product muddy. If you can't hear an instrument, don't necessarily think that increasing the fader level will solve everything. Sometimes reducing the levels of the other tracks is preferable as you are less likely to end up with everything too high and little room for manoeuvre.
Trimming the final mix	Be careful how you trim the beginning and the end of the final mixdown, following the instructions given. The lead in and lead out should be less than one second (unless otherwise stated in the question). Careful positioning of the locators before you export your mix to file will help with this. A long silence is likely to be a problem but it is highly undesirable that any of the music is cut off. Depending on your software, it is sometimes a good idea to re-import the exported file to your software to check for both clean endings and a decent output level with no distortion, or check it with an audio player such as QuickTime.
Metronome and mutes	Make sure you have turned the metronome off and muted any other unwanted audio or MIDI.

Bouncing down/ exporting	When you bounce/export your final mix you will not need to use dither, as all the files supplied by the exam board will have been set at 16 bit /44.1kHz. If you have used a virtual instrument for any MIDI work, this also will be exported as audio. However, if you have used a standard MIDI sound source, perhaps from your computer's soundcard, then this will need to be converted to audio before you bounce down the mix.
Using automation	The application of some processors may require you to use automation.
Left and right	Check that left and right are the right way round.
Volume level	Ensure the overall volume level is appropriate (probably normalised with no clipping).
A final check	It is very easy to leave one track muted accidentally, or bypass the reverb when mixing down in a hurry without noticing, so double check your final mix by listening to the wav file the examiner will be listening to.

Section 3: examples of questions and student responses

How to gain marks

This section will cover how to gain marks for the following type of questions.

- Key musical features
- 'Spot the error' and other notation questions
- Practical questions
- The essay question.

KEY MUSICAL FEATURES

Q: What key is the music in?

Correct answer: A minor

Student answer: A

- This response receives no marks because 'A' is shorthand for A major and is therefore incorrect.
- In general, it is best to be specific for a question on key: clarify the letter name with major or minor as appropriate.

Q: Complete the table below. Identify the notes in each chord, referring to the given example.

C	C E G
G	G B D
E[7]	E G B D♯
Am[7]	A C♯ E G

In the above example, the student scores as follows:

- One mark for the first response; the question is asking you to identify the notes in the triad of G major and would normally be worth only one mark. No marks would be given if any of the three notes were inaccurate.
- No marks for the second response; where an extension to the triad is required then there is normally one mark awarded for the triad and one mark for the extension. In this

case the G should be G♯ (so the triad is inaccurate), and the seventh note would be D, not D♯. If the G♯ had been given correctly, the response would have scored one mark. The third response also scores zero marks; unfortunately, even though the seventh note is given correctly as G, if the triad is incorrect the whole chord is considered to be incorrect.

Q: What musical term best describes how the bass part is played?

Correct answer: legato

Student answer: **ligato**

QWC (quality of written communication) is only assessed in questions indicated with *. In all other questions the examiner will seek to credit any response that is intelligible, even if it is misspelled. You should always try to spell your answers correctly and present your work neatly, but if you make your best attempt at spelling a word you may still gain credit, even if you haven't quite managed to get it completely accurate. In the example above, the student would have been given the one available mark for the question despite the misspelling.

'SPOT THE ERROR' AND OTHER NOTATION QUESTIONS

IDENTIFYING RHYTHMIC ERRORS

*Q: There are **two** rhythm errors in **bars 5–12**. Identify the errors by circling **the entire bar**. Notate the correct rhythm for **the entire bar** on the blank stave above.*

Just by scanning the bold type, it is easy to note what the examiner is after; bars 1–4 and 13 onwards are irrelevant, so you don't need to listen to them for this question. You will lose marks if you note that the mistake is just in the last two beats, circle these notes only and write the correct rhythm in the empty stave; you haven't answered the question correctly. Even though you have spotted the inaccuracy, you are likely to score zero marks. You must circle the **entire bar** and write out the correct rhythm for the **entire bar**.

What mark would you give the following example?

The mistakes are in bar 6 (beats 3 and 4 should be two crotchets) and in bar 11 (beats 1 and 2 should be a single minim).

- The student has correctly identified both errors and has written the correct rhythms in the blank staves.
- However, in bar 6 they have circled and written out only the last two beats of the bar. Therefore, no marks are given.
- In bar 11, the student has circled the entire bar and written out the entire bar correctly in the blank stave.
- Therefore, they have scored two marks out of a possible four.

ERRORS OF PITCH

Questions where you must spot errors of pitch often have a significant difference: they usually require you to circle the incorrect pitch (that is, a **single note**) and to write the correct pitch (again, a single note) in the blank stave provided. However, it may be that there are two errors in one bar and you are asked to write out the whole bar.

- Present your work neatly for notation answers
- If a pitch is ambiguous (i.e. it is not clear whether the note is on a line or in a space) then your answer will receive no credit
- Write out notation in pencil so that it is easy to correct
- If you do use pen and make a mess, make sure that the correct pitch is included as clearly as possible, and then above the note write the letter name of the pitch you have settled on as your final answer.

PRACTICAL QUESTIONS

> Refer to page 86 for a list of topics that might come up in the practical questions. There is more detail on the nuts and bolts of these different effects, processes and techniques in section 1 of this revision guide.

The most important thing to note for these questions is that they are marked on the basis of what the examiner hears on the CD submitted along with your completed exam paper. No matter how much time you have spent on these questions, they cannot be marked without your correctly exported wav file. Also, it is important to note instructions such as 'ensure the metronome is turned off' and 'ensure the track is soloed'. Failure to observe such instructions will disadvantage you considerably.

> Refer to pages 91–3 for more advice.

ESSAY QUESTIONS

Question 4 is the essay question. It is the question that deals directly with Area of Study 3: the development of technology-based music.

> Section 1 of this revision guide goes into detail about what you should learn for each topic that may come up in this question.

Every year there will be a choice of two questions from which you must select one. There is no set pattern of rotation for any particular topic year on year. It is quite possible for a topic that came up one year to come up again in the following year with a completely different slant on it. The one thing you can be sure of is that the two questions will be from different areas.

> It is highly likely that you will feel much more comfortable with one of the options than the other, so go with the area you feel most knowledgeable about. If you are not sure which question to tackle, do a very quick list of points (one or two words per point) that you think might be creditworthy for each question. Go with the question which generates the longer list.

QWC is examined in this question; it is examiner-speak for 'spelling and writing skills'. As such, you must ensure that you use technical, musical and music technology vocabulary where appropriate, but you must also ensure it is used in the correct context and spelled correctly in order to gain the marks. It is possible to gain credit if you misspell a technical term and then go on to describe its function correctly. However, you may gain less credit than you would if you spelled the term correctly in the first place. Similarly, it is important to keep your answer as coherent as possible. Try to deal with points in a logical, concise order, and avoid repetition.

Aside from QWC issues, question 4 is assessed as one mark per creditworthy point you make. There will probably be 80-plus creditworthy points available on the mark scheme. A total of 16 marks are available for this question, so you only need to make 16 of these points in order to score full marks for the question. It is a good idea to write everything you know about the topic. This will give you the opportunity for maximum marks, just in case you are incorrect with several of your points, or there were QWC issues with some of them.

Writing in continuous prose is encouraged, but not absolutely essential. A well-organised bullet list can also showcase your understanding of a topic, so long as it includes enough detail. Remember that quantity does not always equal quality.

You should leave about 15–20 minutes for this question. Start by making a list of all the things you want to say, then organise them into a coherent order. Begin writing after you have spent a few minutes planning: you will not regret a few minutes of planning time, but you may well regret the lack of it. Do not cross out your planning until you are sure you have covered all the points in your essay. If something is not crossed out then an examiner will need to take it into account, but if it is crossed out then it could be thought of as being discarded and thus not taken into account.

The following are examples of what students may have written in response to questions from past papers.

> Ask your teacher for a copy of the mark schemes from previous years so that you can see where the marks for the following examples came from.

Remember not to be too fazed by the level of detail in the mark scheme: it is there for an examiner to be able to give credit for all the possible correct answers, but you are not expected to know absolutely everything that is in it! Any words or phrases underlined are considered creditworthy.

EXAMPLE 1A: FEATURES OF AN ELECTRIC GUITAR AND HOW IT WORKS

The electric guitar has become an iconic symbol of rock music. Players like Jimi Hendrix and Eric Clapton and the blues and jazz players who came before them raised the profile of the electric guitar to legendary status. Current electric guitars are based on Gibson's Les Paul solid body design. Les Paul was a jazz musician who suggested ideas to Gibson so that the guitar could avoid feedback and hum issues. So the first important feature on an electric guitar is a solid body.

The second important feature is the pickup. The pickup picks up the sound of the electric guitar and sends it as a signal. This works by the six magnets being wrapped in copper wire about 15,000 times. When a power supply is added this makes an electric field. When the string vibrates, the vibration is turned into an electronic signal which can then be amplified by an amplifier.

The third important feature is the amplifier. Modern amplifiers can have lots of built-in effects which can be added to the sound of the basic electric guitar to make it more interesting or different. Many guitarists think that valve amplifiers are best because they have a 'warmer' sound, but these are quite expensive and can be fragile. Transister amplifiers are cheaper and often have lots of additional features because their lower price allows these extras to be added in addition to the basic amplifier. Most amplifiers will have distortion and reverb but some will have other effects like chorus and vibrato.

The fourth important feature of an electric guitar is the bridge which connects the strings to the body. Some guitars have very simple bridges that cannot move, but some have Floyd Rose bridges which have whammy bars attached. Whammy bars allow the player to change the pitch of the strings without moving their other hand so that interesting effects can be created such as dive bombs. You can't do dive bombs with a bridge that doesn't move.

- The student here talks about the solid body and then talks about feedback in the next sentence – a close enough link for another credit.
- 'Pickup' is an example of a buzzword – a word that is creditworthy just by mentioning it in the correct context.
- The student here is trying to say something about how pickups work, but is just missing the point and not quite saying anything that is creditworthy. Note that 'electronic' is not creditworthy in the mark scheme, but 'electrical energy' is.
- This student spends a lot of time discussing amplifiers, but amplifiers are not part of the question. You must answer the question given, not the question you would like it to be. There is only one mark available for any discussion of amplifiers and one mark for any discussion of effects, so all this time was wasted.
- Several marks have been picked up for the discussion of Floyd Rose tremolo systems; the student went into some detail on this. If they had gone into similar detail on the other aspects of a guitar's construction, they could have scored a lot more marks.
- Note that 'transister' is spelled incorrectly. If there had been a mark available for mentioning transistor amps, it would have been lost anyway due to QWC.

Total: 12 marks

EXAMPLE 1B: FEATURES OF AN ELECTRIC GUITAR AND HOW IT WORKS

An electric guitar has a number of features that allow the player to control their sound. Although there are many different types of electric guitar, the basic features remain the same for almost all of them. Some important models that have often been copied by other guitar makers are the Fender Telecaster, the Fender Stratocaster and the Gibson Les Paul. All of these guitars, and the guitars that are based on the same designs, are solid bodies. The solid body was introduced by Les Paul to try and avoid the nasty feedback that was hard to avoid with hollow-body guitars like the Gibson ES335. Although the Gibson ES335 is a hollow body guitar, it is still very popular today.

All solid body guitars have pickups because they make very little sound on their own. Pickups are magnets with lots of wire wrapped around them. When there is an electrical current in the wire an electromagnetic field is produced by the pickups. When the metal strings vibrate in the electromagnetic field, a signal is produced. This signal then travels along the lead plugged into the jack input of the guitar and goes to an amplifier where it is amplified to make the sound audible.

The bridge pickup is traditionally louder than the neck pickup. The bridge pickup has a harsher tone than the neck pickup and is often used for soloing. A pickup selector switch allows the player to control their sound by selecting one pickup or a mix of different pickups. A volume control allows the player to adjust their volume without running backwards and forwards to the amplifier, and a tone control allows the player to reduce the treble. Sometimes on some guitars there is a volume control and a tone control for each individual pickup which gives the player even more options.

Some guitars like the Fender Stratocaster make noise when they are amplified because of the types of pickups used. The pickups in a Fender Stratocaster are called single coil pickups because they have just one magnet in them. Guitars like the Gibson Les Paul have humbucker pickups. These are two single-coil pickups put together. The two pickups detect the same signal, but they are wired to cancel out the interference.

Different players like different types of pickups in their guitars because they want to produce a certain type of sound. Guitarists who play metal will want to use humbuckers and guitarists who play funk will want to use single coil pickups. There are lots of different pickups available to buy today so you can even change them in your own guitar yourself without having to buy a new instrument.

- This response has well over the maximum 16 creditworthy points. It is a well constructed essay that has benefitted from some planning time. There are several major points missed out, such as discussion of the bridge and other important aspects of a guitar's construction, but the points that are dealt with are covered in enough detail to attract a lot of marks. This goes to show that you are often able to approach a question from several different angles and still gain good marks.
- Although there are no marks available for naming specific guitar types (there are a couple of marks for 'Les Paul' and 'Fender', but these were for reasons other than being specific guitar makes/models), there is no harm in mentioning what you know in passing, just in case there were. This is true of any topic: if you know any model names and/or numbers, do mention them where appropriate in case there is a clause in the mark scheme such as 'give one mark maximum for mentioning specific examples'. There may even be one mark for each specific example, depending on how the question is worded, so feel free to demonstrate the depth of your knowledge!

Total: 16 marks (max.)

EXAMPLE 2A: DIGITAL SAMPLERS – WHAT THEY ARE AND HOW THEY HAVE DEVELOPED FROM THE 1980S ONWARDS?

- A sample is a snippet of sound
- It can be played or looped
- We can load samples into a sampler
- Samplers are software nowadays
- In the 1980s it would have been done with hardware played into the mixing desk
- Reason is an example of a software sampler
- Samples are used in lots of today's music
- With the evolution of Cubase and other computer programs, samplers have become more powerful
- A sample could be a four-bar phrase from a song that is used to create another song
- Samplers have gone from hardware to software
- A sampler can hold many samples.

- This is an example of an essay arranged as bullet points. Unfortunately, the brevity of the response is not made up for by high quality content.
- A little more detail was required on the 'software sampler' point; an accurate example should have been given. Giving 'Reason' as an example shows a misunderstanding of software samplers since Reason is a much more complex piece of software that hosts sampler plug-ins rather than being just a sampler itself.
- The rest of the response does not contain any information that answers the question, without repeating previous creditworthy information.

Total: 3 marks

EXAMPLE 2B: DIGITAL SAMPLERS – WHAT THEY ARE AND HOW THEY HAVE DEVELOPED FROM THE 1980S ONWARDS?

A sampler is a piece of equipment that stores previously recorded audio in RAM (random access memory), ready for instant playback. A keyboard is normally used to trigger the sampler to play back the samples. If you play higher up the keyboard the sample will sound higher in pitch; if you play lower down, the sample will sound lower in pitch. This means that lots of different notes can be played using one single sample, but if you play too many different notes using just the one sample, the highest and lowest notes will sound very odd. Because of this, people tend to map lots of different samples to the different notes on the keyboard to avoid the 'chipmunk' sound. Each key can be assigned a different sample, and even lots of samples depending on how hard you hit the key (this is called velocity layering).

The first sampler was developed in the 1970s and was called the Melatron. It was very expensive, so only quite famous bands could afford it. As the digital age rose samplers became much more affordable and popular in the 1980s. One of the first samplers was the EMU Emulator. These samplers were not very powerful and could only use short samples because memory was so expensive in those days and floppy discs had to be used. As the technology improved, longer and higher quality samples could be recorded and played back – even large portions of individual songs.

Samplers contain controls similar to those on subtractive synthesisers such as filters, envelope generators and LFOs so that the samples can be manipulated after they have been recorded. Some synthesisers even use samples so that they can create more realistic sounding instruments instead of those that can be created using subtractive synthesis or FM.

In the 2000s samplers moved onto computers so that they are now software instead of hardware. This means that it is possible to store whole orchestras and very detailed samples of pianos that take many GBs of storage space. It also means that it is much easier to manipulate the samples because it can all be done on a computer screen instead of a tiny LCD screen, and you can use the computer mouse and keyboard instead of just a few buttons on the hardware. NI Kontakt is an example of a modern software sampler that gives many ways to manipulate the samples. It is even possible to buy many different banks of samples online or on DVD that can then be loaded into Kontakt without having to be edited first.

- A reasonably detailed response that really hits the target; it includes lots of accurate information and is organised chronologically.
- Reference to the Mellotron is irrelevant because the question asks about digital samplers. Also, since the word was spelled incorrectly, it would not have gained any credit anyway.
- It would have been good if this student had made some mention of sample rates and/or bit depths to accompany the discussion of memory restrictions. Follow your thoughts through to their logical conclusion and explain everything fully, in order to access marks you may not have been aware were available.
- Although the student has made four creditworthy points on similarities to analogue synths, a maximum of three points was available for this in the mark scheme.
- Note that some sentences mention something and go on to explain it, managing to pick up several marks just because they mentioned several points in the mark scheme almost by accident. This is a benefit of answering in full sentences rather than in bullet points.

Total: 16 marks (max.)

EXAMPLE 3A: MICROPHONES – WHAT DO THEY DO, HOW DO DYNAMIC AND CONDENSER MICROPHONES WORK, AND WHAT ARE THE BENEFITS OF EACH TYPE OF MICROPHONE?

The dynamic microphone is mainly used for the drums or the guitar amplifiers, and the condenser microphone is powered by phantom power which is then used for vocals, acoustic guitar and piano. A dynamic microphone does not need phantom power. A condenser is normally clearer so it is best for the vocalists. Dynamics are more robust than the condensers, so they are best for <u>micing instruments that are very loud</u> and need them near to them like the drums where the drummer plays loudly and might hit the mics by accident. Condenser mics are less strong than dynamics so they would be used for softer sounds.

▪ This is a very short answer, which may have been completed in a hurry. However, it still manages to use a few buzzwords and also make some valid points.

Total: 4 marks

EXAMPLE 3B: MICROPHONES – WHAT DO THEY DO, HOW DO DYNAMIC AND CONDENSER MICROPHONES WORK AND WHAT ARE THE BENEFITS OF EACH TYPE OF MICROPHONE?

▪ Microphones <u>convert sound waves into electrical current</u>
▪ When the sound is converted to an electrical current it is passed through a preamp so that it can be heard
▪ Dynamic and condenser mics have different benefits and drawbacks
▪ Condenser mics are more fragile than dynamics
▪ Condensers feature a <u>moving capacitor plate</u> (they are sometimes called capacitor mics because of this feature). The plate is very thin, <u>so high frequencies can be picked up much more accurately</u> than for dynamic mics. The sounds <u>push the plate in and out</u> and this causes a signal to travel down the lead
▪ The benefits of a condenser microphone are:
  ▪ <u>Flat frequency response</u>
  ▪ <u>More sensitive</u>
  ▪ <u>Good signal to noise ratio</u>
  ▪ Better capture of high frequencies
▪ Condenser mics need <u>phantom power</u> (48V) to <u>charge the plate</u>
▪ Small diaphram condensers are used for <u>capturing transients</u>
▪ Dynamic mics work by the sound <u>moving a coil</u> that is <u>inside a magnetic field</u>. This <u>makes a small current flow</u> which needs to be amplified by a preamp
▪ The benefits of a dynamic microphone are:
  ▪ It is <u>robust</u>
  ▪ It is <u>cheap to make</u>
  ▪ It is often used on stage rather than in the studio
  ▪ It can <u>handle loud SPLs</u> (sound pressure levels)
  ▪ It is <u>resistant to moisture</u> and often comes with a spit guard
▪ A popular example of a dynamic mic is the Shure SM58, which is often used by rock vocalists because it has a mid frequency boost
▪ Because of the thickness of the diaphram and the way it moves, dynamic mics aren't so good at picking up high frequencies
▪ Dynamic mics are usually <u>cardioid</u> or hypercardioids.

▪ This is a good example of a high-scoring bullet point response. As with the other high-scoring responses, this answer has been well organised with a logical flow of information. It looks like the student has made a list and has then slightly expanded on the language to make it suitable as an extended response.

- 'Through a preamp so that it can be heard' – it would be better if the technical reason was given for the use of a preamp, as this would have been creditworthy whereas 'so that it can be heard' is not enough.
- This student stuck to the benefits of each type of microphone, thus answering the question correctly. Listing the drawbacks of each type of microphone would not have been creditworthy, even if the information given was correct, because it would not have answered the question.
- 'Condenser mics need phantom power (48V)' – the simple addition of the '(48V)' is worth an extra mark. If you know some technical information, give it in your response, even if it seems totally obvious and basic to you.
- 'Diaphram' is misspelled, so attracts no marks.
- While there was no additional credit for naming specific microphones, it did not do any harm to mention them, just in case.

Total: 16 marks (max.)

Section 4: top ten tips for success in your exam

1. Attempt the questions in the order 1–2–3–5–4. This way you will be completing all the practical tasks first without having a break in between. Also, if you run out of time for question 4 you might be able to scribble a few hurried thoughts quickly, gaining 5 or 6 marks. However, if you run out of time before you export your mix for question 5 then you lose all 18 marks. Another benefit of this approach is that if you have a few minutes at the end of the exam you can go back to your mix for question 5 and listen to it with slightly fresher ears to check that you are happy with it.

2. Double check the location of your saved audio files and check that they are what you think they should be – the exam paper is crystal clear as to what you should name your files. It is important your technician can find your files easily so your CD can be burnt. This is particularly important if your centre runs the exam in multiple sittings.

3. Check that the correct parts are muted/unmuted before you export the audio files for questions 1–3. Make sure the metronome is muted before exporting audio files if asked to do so.

4. If there is a question involving some element of audio editing or looping, make sure that the loops are glitch-free.

5. Take a few minutes to organise your thoughts and structure your essay before you begin writing your response to question 4.

6. Always make more than 16 points in question 4 just in case some of your points are inaccurate or include some misspelled vocabulary.

7. Use a pencil for any questions involving notation or diagrams so that you can rub out any errors easily. You may want to go over the final answer in black pen.

8. Learn your vocabulary. Keep a list of musical, technical and music technology vocabulary and commit it to memory. Using the correct technical term is often worth more marks than not doing so.

9. Have a go at as many past papers as you can, using the same equipment you will be using for your actual exam. Get used to the foibles of the equipment you have to use so that you can spend your time efficiently in the exam.

10. Check that your headphones are the right way around by experimenting with the pan controls on your DAW.

Further resources

Useful websites

The following websites provide useful additional information:

www.soundonsound.com
The most comprehensive of the British industry magazines. Click on articles and search your subject.

www.mixonline.com
Excellent American recording industry trade magazine with lots of articles.

www.sweetwater.com/expert-center
Commercial outlet but provides lots of technical knowledge, including featured articles and an excellent glossary.

www.tweakheadz.com
Useful information for home and project studio users.

www.vintagesynth.com
A very good site for an overview of synthesisers. The interactive timeline under the resources tab is particularly helpful.

www.midi.org
For all technical MIDI matters.

www.indiana.edu/%7Eemusic/alldocs.htm
Excellent university funded site with well-explained articles.

Background reading

The following books provide additional useful information:

Martin: *Edexcel Music Technology AS/A2 Study Guide, second edition* (Rhinegold Education, 2009)

Charlton and Boulton: *Edexcel Music Technology AS/A2 Listening Tests, second edition* (Rhinegold Education, 2010)

Huber and Runstein: *Modern Recording Techniques, seventh edition* (Focal Press, 2009)

Bartlett and Bartlett: *Practical Recording Techniques: The Step-by-Step Approach to Professional Audio Recording, sixth edition* (Focal Press, 2012)

Davis and Jones: *The Sound Reinforcement Handbook, second edition* (Hal Leonard Corporation, 1990)

Buick and Leonard: *Music Technology Reference Book* (PC Publishing, 1994)

Cutchin and Macdonald: *The Illustrated Home Recording Handbook, revised edition* (Flame Tree Publishing, 2007)

Pejrolo. A: *Creative Sequencing Techniques for Music Production: A Practical Guide to Pro Tools, Logic, Digital Performer, and Cubase, second edition* (Focal Press, 2011)

Glossary

ADAT Stands for Alesis Digital Audio Tape. It records eight tracks digitally on a standard $\frac{1}{2}$" SVHS video cassette.

Additive synthesis A synthesis technique that combines sine waves of various pitches to produce a new timbre. Used in Hammond organs.

Amplitude The height of a waveform – the higher the level the louder the sound.

Analogue Continually changing voltage or current that represents a sound – the representation of the sound is analogous to the original sound wave.

Attack 1) The initial portion of a sound – the time taken for a sound to reach its maximum amplitude.
2) The time taken for a processor to act after the signal has passed a set threshold.

Auto-tune Processors that adjust and correct the pitch of audio recordings according to preset templates.

Aux (auxiliary) A line split away from the channel in a mixing desk for the purpose of routing a portion of the signal to effects or other mix outputs.

Balance The volume of instruments or parts relative to each other.

Bit depth The number of bits available to describe a number. The more bits, the more resolution will be available. For example, four bits will allow 16 different values, while 16 bits will allow 65,536 different values. In audio, a lower bit depth produces *grainy* audio because the steps between one value and another become audible.

Bus or Buss A common electrical signal path along which signals may travel.

Codec A codec (compression/decompression or coder/decoder) is a software component that is used for compressing and decompressing data. Commonly used for audio and video.

Compression 1) Squeezing together molecules in the air
2) Automatic reduction of the dynamic range of a sound
3) Reducing the amount of data in a file

Cut-off frequency The nominal value at which a filter has an audible effect on the frequency range of a sound. Normally applied to low-pass filters, in which case the cut-off frequency describes the highest audible frequency.

CV/gate Control voltage/gate: used in analogue systems as a means of controlling external devices from a sequencer. The control voltage usually controls the pitch, and the gate (sometimes called the trigger) controls the note on/off.

DAW Digital Audio Workstation: refers to a system to record, edit and manipulate digital audio. It can be hardware or software.

Delay An effect in which the original signal is repeated one or more times. There is normally a progressive decrease in the volume and the high frequency content with each repeat.

Dither Audio tool used when reducing from a high bit-depth to 16 bit CD quality to maximise the quality of the sound.

Echo chamber A large, enclosed space with hard surfaces used to create echoes and reverberation.

Envelope In audio recording software this refers to the way in which the level of a sound or signal varies over time. Important in sound synthesis where the envelope's ADSR refers to attack, decay, sustain and release parameters of a sound over time. Can be applied to timbre and pitch as well as the more usual loudness.

Frequency The rate per second at which an oscillating body vibrates. Usually measured in Hertz (Hz).

Frequency modulation 1) Where the frequency of a carrier signal is varied in accordance with a modulating signal. In audio, the carrier and the modulating signal are both in the audible frequency range, creating a complex waveform.
2) Changing pitch or vibrato.

FX Short for 'effects'. Processes applied to a signal to alter its sound quality in some way, or the devices used to do so.

Gain The stage of a pre-amplifier that boosts the level of a signal at the beginning of the signal path. A term commonly applied to any volume boost in the signal path.

General MIDI (GM) An agreed standard to ensure compatibility between MIDI equipment manufacturers. The term is now often used just to refer to the agreed list of 128 voices in the GM soundset or to the agreed standard for a set of drum/percussion sounds contained within MIDI compatible sound sources.

Harmonics A frequency that is a whole-number multiple of the fundamental frequency. A series of harmonics is present, sounding quietly as overtones to a natural sound, and contributing to its timbre.

Harmoniser An 'intelligent' pitch-shifter; it follows the pitch of the input audio and adds another pitch, taken from a pre-selected key/scale. Harmonisers will usually be able to add several different notes from the chosen key/scale. Vocalists will often use these devices when performing live to create the illusion of several singers.

Latency Refers to the delay produced by computer circuitry when trying to monitor audio signals after input.

LFO Low frequency oscillator: normally applied to a signal to modulate it in some way.

Loop A repeated passage. Often used to refer to samples that are imported into a sequence and repeated.

MIDI Musical Instrument Digital Interface: an 8-bit computer language developed to allow electronic musical instruments to communicate with each other and the hardware necessary to facilitate this communication.

Modular synth A synthesiser made up of separate sections (such as oscillators, filters and envelope generators) that are linked together by signal cables.

Modulation Anything that changes over a time period - in traditional music it refers to key but in Music Technology it can be applied to audio parameters such as frequency and amplitude.

Monophonic 1) A word used to describe a musical texture in which there is only one part.
2) A synthesiser capable of playing only one note at a time is called a monophonic synthesiser.

MTC Midi Time Code.

Normalization An automatic process available in most audio software whereby the gain of the music is adjusted so the peak level will just arrive at 0dB.

Omni-Directional Microphones receiving sound evenly from all directions.

Overdub One or more previously recorded tracks are monitored whilst simultaneously recording one or more signals onto other tracks.

Pan The placement of sound in the stereo field.

Pickup This device is a transducer that captures mechanical vibrations and converts them to electrical signals using electromagnetism.

Plug-in A computer program written to produce or manipulate audio within an existing audio sequencing package.

Polar response A pattern that shows how sensitive a microphone is to signals arriving from different angles.

Polyphonic 1) A word used to describe a musical texture in which two or more musical strands are heard simultaneously.
2) A synthesiser capable of playing more than one note at a time is called a polyphonic synthesiser.

Q The range of frequencies affected by a filter – a measure of the resonance of a filter.

Quantisation noise Noise produced from an error or rounding off the smooth analogue waveform into the multiple steps needed for digital information during the analogue to digital conversion process.

Ratio A parameter on compressors used to set by how much a signal is reduced after it passes the threshold level.

Release 1) The final portion of a sound – the time taken for a sound to decay after the note has been released. 2) The time taken for a processor to stop acting after the signal has passed a set threshold.

Resonance control Used in synthesizers – this increases the gain immediately around the cut-off frequency.

Sample A short, pre-recorded sound used in the context of a piece of music, or a digital recording of a naturally occurring sound.

Sample rate The number of times an analogue to digital converter samples the signal every second, measured in Hertz (e.g. 44,100 times per second = 44.1kHz).

Sequencer The computer package/hardware device used to facilitate the input and editing of MIDI data. Most sequencers are capable of combining MIDI data and audio and are called audio sequencers.

Side-chain A portion of the main signal that is separated out to be processed in some way. Some processors (such as compressors) use the side-chain to control when they act.

SMPTE Society of Motion Picture and Television Engineers; sophisticated time code used to lock magnetic tape for purposes of synchronization.

Solo monitoring When depressed this button on a mixing desk will mute all other signals except the chosen one.

Spot mic The technique of focusing a microphone on an individual or small group within a larger group that is being captured by other microphones so as to allow for selective boosting of the signal.

Standing waves Low frequency resonances that take place between two parallel reflecting wall surfaces.

Subtractive synthesis Sound synthesis technique that creates new sounds by filtering out components from a richer waveform.

Threshold A preset point which, once passed, causes a process to occur. Used in, for example, compressors and gates.

Tonewheel A series of disks rotated by a motor in proximity to an electromagnetic pickup.

Triggering To cause an event to begin. To trigger a sample is to start the sample playing.

Valve amplifiers Amplifiers that use vacuum tubes (valves) instead of transistors in the pre-amp and/ or power amp stages. These are often felt to give a 'warmer' sound.

Virtual modelling Creating a software version of a hardware device.

XLR A 3-pin male/female connector that is commonly used to carry balanced analogue audio signals for microphones.